O² X̄

CAPTIVE FLAMES

A COLLECTION OF PANEGYRICS
BY THE RIGHT REVEREND MONSIGNOR
RONALD KNOX

May, 1941, selection of the
SPIRITUAL BOOK ASSOCIATES
with the permission of
BURNS OATES : LONDON

NIHIL OBSTAT:
EDUARDUS CAN. MAHONEY, S.TH.D.,
Censor deputatus.

IMPRIMATUR:
E. MORROGH BERNARD,
Vicarius Generalis.

WESTMONASTERII,
die 13a Julii 1940.

DEDICATION

TO

ARNOLD LUNN

DEAR ARNOLD,

You are always complaining that I do not give you copies of my books ; so I have determined to manœuvre for a superior position by dedicating this to you. You will complain at once that a collection of old sermons is a poor sort of book, hardly a book at all. To be sure, nothing is more dated than your old sermons—especially occasional sermons, like these. Their associations were local, the impulse of ecclesiastical festivity which inspired them is not easily recaptured ; your own style, your own taste, have changed, and these past utterances hardly seem to belong to you. Besides, what is not dated, that was written between 1919 and 1939 ? Those two decades of our lives will perhaps be remembered in history only as an uneasy twilight ; we cannot tell, whether of dusk or dawn.

And yet, though all the setting of these sermons be fugitive, the main theme of them is something which does not alter with our shifting perspectives, does not grow old. The saints do not belong to a period ; there is a cousinship between St. Cecily talking to the angel Valerian could not see, and St. Bernadette kneeling at the foot of the rock, apparently all alone. They are fixed stars, not subject to any law of impermanence. And this book is about saints ; a puddle

reflecting their star-shine. Only, I found that I had
included one about Henry the Sixth, who was never
canonized, in the hope that he would not arouse any
Harrovian prejudice in you ; and one about Roger
Bacon, no saint but an Oxford scientist—I know you
are patient with scientists, and Oxford has a meaning
for you. So I thought I would round off the number
of these sermons, for luck, with the sermon I think I
am most proud to have preached ; the panegyric
uttered in Westminster Cathedral, when you and I and
all our contemporaries lost, in Chesterton, the oracle
of our youth.

One of the sermons was preached to undergraduates
(you have preached to undergraduates) ; several to
schoolboys ; not all of them, therefore, have the
dignity which some people associate with the pulpit.
But I put them in, leaving them just as they were, in
the hope that one or two people might pick up the
book here and there, who had been present when one
of those sermons was delivered, and so cheat themselves
for a moment with the illusion of living in the past.
That, for all men, is a transitory relief ; though their
memory does not go back to such fine days as ours.

Such as it is, then, here it is ; and never say that
I did not dedicate a book to you.

R. A. K.

ALDENHAM

CONTENTS

If a star were confined into a tomb,
  Her captive flames must needs burn there;
But when the hand, that locked her up, gives room,
  She'll shine through all the sphere.

HENRY VAUGHAN.

I. ST. CECILIA

(Preached at St. Anselm and St. Cecilia's, Kingsway.)

In like manner also, let wives be subject to their husbands : that, if any believe not the word, they may be won without the word, by the conversation of the wives, considering your chaste conversation with fear. 1 *Peter* iii, 1.

THE legends of the early Roman Saints, among whom your holy patroness St. Cecilia is numbered, do not always command great attention from the critically minded historian. The records, he will tell you, were compiled at an uncertain date, but a date very much later than the events they deal with ; the miracles in them are purposelessly elaborate ; the tone of them rather suggests that they have been written up for the edification of pious readers. That is all very well, but every now and again you meet with curious evidences of the accuracy of these Roman traditions, and not least in the case of St. Cecilia herself. A little time ago they dug underneath the Church of St. Cecilia across the Tiber, to find out whether there was any justification for the tradition that that church was built on the site of St. Cecilia's house. And sure enough it proved that St. Cecilia's, like St. Clement's, was built over an old Roman house. But there was more than that—there is one chapel in the church which was always supposed to be the exact site of St. Cecilia's martyrdom. In the story, you will remember, St. Cecilia was finally put to death in a bath. And just underneath the chapel of the martyrdom, so I am told, in the structure of the old Roman house, they found the traces of the old Roman apparatus for heating the bath water. Which shows that we ought to be very careful about how we disbelieve the Roman legends.

But whether the story of St. Cecilia as it is told in her acts is all true or only partly true, there is a simplicity about the whole story and a simplicity about St. Cecilia's character in the story which demands that anyone who stands in the pulpit on an occasion like this should preach a simple sermon about her. She is not like that other great Virgin Martyr, St. Catherine of Alexandria. St. Catherine of Alexandria was a great philosopher, according to the story, who confounded all the thinkers of Alexandria by the acuteness of her apologetics. And, though I have every respect for St. Catherine as the patroness of my own College, I do imagine St. Catherine as a rather formidable person to meet ; she would, I fancy, lecture on Catholic Evidence platforms. But there is nothing of that about St. Cecilia, although she is full of zeal for her religion ; her public is the home, her platform the breakfast table. I hope it is not necessary to remind you, except in the most general way, of her story—how she was married to a young pagan called Valerian, but persuaded him to respect her vow of virginity, because her guardian Angel would make him sorry for it if he did otherwise : how Valerian wanted to see this guardian Angel, but Cecilia, with her innocent craft, said he could not do that unless he was baptized first ; how he was baptized, and saw the Angel at her side as she prayed ; how he made a convert of his brother Tiburtius, and how first the two brothers, and then Cecilia herself, were punished with death for professing the Christian religion. It is an old story, and a familiar one : and while we do all homage to St. Catherine for her courage in lecturing in the parks, we shall always need St. Cecilia as well, quietly working at home for the conversion of her own husband and his family.

Not that St. Cecilia herself was in the position of a modern wife. Like so many Christian ladies of her time, she had taken, in imitation of our Blessed Lady, a vow of perpetual virginity. When you read of the Virgin Martyrs you must not think of that connection of titles as an accidental one ; that certain martyrs happened to be virgins or certain virgins happened to be martyrs. They were martyrs because they were virgins : it was because they insisted on keeping their vow when their parents wished them to marry that the secret of their attachment to the Christian faith was discovered ; and it was their persistency in maintaining it that led to their martyrdom. It would be hard to estimate, I think, how much of its unpopularity in Roman society the Christian faith owed to its tradition of virginity. You know the horror the world feels when somebody becomes a Catholic ; you know the horror the world feels when somebody goes into a convent : combine those two, and transplant them into a society which is heathen and regards the Christian religion as a dangerous and debased cult and you will realize what the pagans thought of a resolution like St. Cecilia's.

Virginity is an ideal which the pagans had no right to misunderstand. For, in theory, they, too, honoured it ; and it should have commended itself to their heathen instinct for sacrifice. For the point of a sacrifice is that the victim should be spotless, the best of its kind. You must offer not what you can well afford to spare, but what will cost you something. The victim must be young, not old, perfect, not mutilated ; pure bred, not of inferior stock : it is the fairest flower that must wither in front of the statue. That is the pagan idea of sacrifice ; and the Christian idea of sacrifice is based on the same principle. In order to give up something to God, we forgo, not the sinful pleasures which we have no right to in any case, but the lawful pleasures which he has given us to enjoy if we will. And it is not broken hearts or wasted careers that produce vocations to the religious life. It is the young, the attractive, the brilliant, those who have the fullest life and the highest hopes before them, who make the perfect sacrifice when they devote themselves to Almighty God in holy religion.

The pagans ought to have understood that ; our modern world does not ; it simply talks about waste. Well, I am not going to argue that now : I am only pointing out that Catholics, in whatever age of the world, must think of the life of virginity as the highest vocation of all. But for this morning, let us think of St. Cecilia rather as an example to people living in the world, a patroness of the home. Hers was a mixed marriage ; of course, she could not help herself ; parents in her day had all the arrangement of such matters in their hands, and presumably her parents were not Christians. Do not let us run away with the impression that all Catholics ought to make mixed marriages, in order to bring fresh families into the Church. There is at least as much harm done to the Church by mixed marriages as good ; at least as much harm. And there is no doubt that, in the eyes of the Church, such marriages are an unfortunate necessity that you cannot avoid, not an ideal to be aimed at. A Catholic who means to marry, but has not (so to speak) filled in the name yet, ought to mean, God willing, to marry a Catholic. But mixed marriages, I suppose, will always go on ; and at any rate we have to allow for the case where, after marriage, the husband or the wife becomes a convert, but not both. The same situation arises—a difference of creed within the four walls of the same house. And it is there that St. Cecilia ought to help us.

What won her husband to the faith, in spite of his passion, in spite (you might almost say) of his love for her, was the purity of her nature which, though a heathen, he could already discern. His eyes were not yet open to the supernatural world that rules and interpenetrates ours; he could not see the Angel until he was baptized. But he could see, in his Christian bride, a new experience in his life—a blinding flash of purity. And the first duty of a Catholic wife or a Catholic husband, if they would redeem the promise they made to labour for husband's or for wife's conversion, is to be a model of Christian purity. The religious life, the life of virginity, is not for them; they have made their choice. But within the holy bond of matrimony, the Catholic has to hold up the highest possible standard of faithfulness—faithfulness both to the person of the other partner in the marriage, and to the will of God in designing matrimony for the procreation of children. Let husband or wife be won to the faith by the behaviour of wife or husband, by considering the chasteness of that behaviour with fear. The world knows that Catholics have a high standard of purity. But the world is not going to be impressed unless it is assured that Catholics keep it.

And that is not only a lesson for wives and husbands; it is a lesson for all of us. The purity which is our traditional inheritance as Catholics has a message and a charm for the world about us. Each of us, whether he likes it or not, is an advertisement of the Catholic faith to the little circle of his neighbours—a good advertisement, or a bad advertisement. And it is such a mistake to think that we ought to try and impress

our neighbours by making it clear to them that
Catholics are not Puritans, are not strait-laced, are
sportsmen like anybody else. The world is very ready
to say that of us, but it does not really respect us for
it. It does not respect us, for being ready to join in
rather risky conversation, and enjoy rather doubtful
jokes ; it does not respect us for being careless about
what company we keep and what places of amusement
we go to. It respects us, if it sees that we shrink from
the touch of anything that may defile us ; if it sees
that the virginity which is practised in the cloister has
its complement and its fruit in the chaste conversation
of Catholics who are living in the world.

So, while St. Anselm's feast reminds us to be loyal
sons of the Church, ready to hold the faith and to
defend the faith in life and in death, let St. Cecilia's
feast remind us to take our Christian vocation
seriously, to follow out in our lives the words we
profess with our lips. And may both, English bishop
and Roman maiden, pray for you who worship here and
for those who minister to you, that when Christ, the
Master they served, comes again in judgement, you
may be found blameless before Almighty God.

II. ST. GEORGE

All mirth is forsaken ; the joy of the land is gone away. *Isaias* xxiv, 11.

WE are celebrating to-night the Feast of St. George,
the heavenly patron of England. I do not mean
to derive any lesson from the life or from the martyrdom of St. George, because it appears that nothing
whatever is known about either. We were all brought
up on the story of St. George and the Dragon, but

these historians who spoil all our nursery romances tell us that this is quite untrue : indeed, the Church has very prudently refrained from giving any sanction to the legend of the Saint, and has officially declared him to be one of those holy men whose actions are known only to God. Instead, we will occupy ourselves this evening in thinking about England. I say England, not the United Kingdom, or the British Empire. St. George is not the patron of the United Kingdom, or of the British Empire. He is the patron of these strange folk that live between the Severn and the Wash, between the Tweed and the English Channel ; a folk honest, on the whole, kindly, on the whole, shy, a little surly, law-abiding, but doggedly tenacious of their rights, rather too self-satisfied, incurably sentimental, dreadfully muddle-headed. He is the patron of that country of chalk downs, of little fields bordered by green hedges, of wandering lanes, of hills scarcely rising above the level of cultivation, of old trees and of long manorial tenure, which we call England. I do not flatter myself by supposing that this congregation consists of entirely English stock ; I conceive it to be probable that there are one or two of you, scattered about here and there, whose blood thrills to a different music, whose loyalties have their focus on the other side of that channel which we have so strangely dedicated to St. George. I cannot help that ; you are a month late for St. Patrick's Day. You will have to be honorary Englishmen for this evening.

It is a peculiarity of the English that they do most things in a vague, haphazard, untidy sort of way, without being able to give any particular reasons for doing it. And nothing is more characteristic of them than their choice of a patron saint. There was no conceivable reason why it should have been St. George

more than anybody else. There is no ground for
thinking that St. George had ever been in England ;
it is not even certain, I suppose, that he had ever
heard of England. He was represented in popular
legend as being a soldier, but England is not, and
never was, a military nation by choice. We just
picked him up, somehow, in the Crusades, and that
was all there was to it. I doubt, even, whether there
was a great popular devotion to the Saint in the
Middle Ages. A fairly large number of parish churches
are dedicated to him, but not many, I think, date
beyond the Reformation. And I could show you a
list of one hundred and fifty country people in the
later Middle Ages out of whom only three bear George
as their baptismal name. Its real popularity, I fancy,
dates from those one hundred and seventeen continuous years of English history during which George
was the King's name.

But there is one phrase we all of us know which does,
in a curious way, identify our national Saint with the
memory of our remote forefathers, I mean the war cry,
the slogan we should call it : ' Saint George for merry
England ! ' For *merry* England—when I say that there
is no trace of a popular medieval devotion to the Saint,
I must admit on the other side the great popularity of
The George and Dragon as a sign over inn doors.
In that most essentially English of our institutions, the
country inn, our national Saint does seem to have
come to his own. He has passed, somehow, into that
tradition of hearty good-fellowship, of beef-eating and
beer-drinking jollity, of which Chaucer first hymned
the praises, and Charles Dickens wrote the epitaph.
Merry England—it is hard to see why they should
have been so merry. The country was devastated by
wars, civil wars mostly ; the great plague of the
Black Death made whole tracts of the country-side

into a wilderness; there were cruel landlords, there were worldly priests, there was poverty, and loose living, and crime. But, somehow, to these forefathers of ours, the England for which they fought was a merry England; it smiled to them across the seas, as they fell at Crécy and Agincourt, in a haze of fun and good comradeship.

Merry England—do we talk much about 'merry England' now? If you open your morning paper, and cast your eye down the news—strikes, divorce actions, murders, unemployment statistics, grave warnings to the public, and similar matter that chiefly occupy its pages—is merry the first word that rises to your lips? Oh, I know, we are gay, we are frivolous, we hurl ourselves into our pleasures. No expense can be too heavy for producing a film, for putting on a revue, for hiring a football professional. We dance all night, and play tennis all day—those of us who have the leisure. But is there not something suspicious about this feverish gaiety of ours, about these demands for a brighter London, this dreary cry for the unsexing of women, these lurid posters that herald our public amusements? Does not our laughter ring rather hollow, as if we were making merry not because we feel light-hearted, but because we want to forget the anxieties that are weighing us down? Our industries, our trade, our empire, our birth-rate, our morals—do they encourage merriment? Our poetry, our clever novels, our art—do they reflect a mood of happiness? Our expert critics, do they bid us believe that all is well with England? Is our gaiety real, or is it a smile painted on the face of a corpse?

Oh, I am not going to talk politics. I am not going to discuss how much of our present difficulties we owe to our ancestors, how much to ourselves, how much to circumstances that we could not have avoided. Even at this moment it is doubtful whether our merry England will have a merry month of May. It is no place of mine, here, to discuss such issues, unless perhaps to implore your prayers for the divine guidance of our rulers. I will not even remind you—the theme has become almost a trite one—how the landlordism that was born with the Reformation prepared the way for that terrible division of class interests which has been with us since the industrial revolution. I do not believe that in the last resort the moods of a country, its moods of depression, or of elation, of hope, or of despair, arise from economic causes or can be altered by material changes. Outward conditions do affect us, of course—a little at all times, violently at some times. But in the long run England will not be merry or sad because there is more coal or less coal, because there is more trade or less trade. Ultimately the spirit of man is the arbiter of his happiness ; men will be merry or sad according as they have found their right place or their wrong place in the scheme of things ; and peace between nations, peace between classes, will come only when man is at peace with himself, and at peace with God.

And England will not be merry until England is Catholic. That word ' merry ' is not so simple as it sounds. It is a difficult word, for example, to translate into any foreign language. It is typical of our modern conditions that we hardly ever use it nowadays, except when we call a person ' merry,' meaning that he was slightly drunk. It survives, chiefly, in old-fashioned formulas such as Merry England, or a Merry Christmas. Merry does not mean drunk, or uproarious, or frivolous. It means that a man is light-hearted, that his mind is at ease, that he is in a good humour, that he is ready to share a bit of fun with his neighbours. There is humility in the word, and innocence, and comradeship.

And such a frame of mind as that is not to be secured, by grown-up people, through a continuous whirl of excitements, or a long course of dissipations. It comes from within.

A country cannot be merry while it forgets God. And a country cannot be merry for long, or with safety, if it tries to be Christian without being Catholic. England is not, of course, even to-day, a country of atheists. But there is a very large fraction of our fellow-countrymen—I do not think you can put it much lower than four-fifths—which does not go to Church. And most of these people do not think about God if they can help it—that is what I call 'forgetting God.' They try to satisfy themselves with this world ; and that is a thing which you cannot do ; Almighty God does not mean us to do it ; he wants to draw us back to himself. The man who confines his outlook to this world is worried all the time, at the back of his mind, by the old riddle of existence ; the troubles, the sufferings, the tragedies of the world keep flicking him like briers as he goes along : problems of conduct— which is the right thing to do, and why should I do it ?—stick to him like burrs and force themselves upon his notice. You may forget your cares for a time, you may drown them occasionally with your pleasures, but you can never banish them. A man will never be light-hearted in this world unless he is thinking of the next world ; this world is too chequered an affair for that.

And in the long run, even a Christian nation cannot be merry unless it is a Catholic nation. For these non-Catholic Christianities—why, I do not know, but as a matter of observation it is true—always go hand-in-hand with some kind of Puritanism that interferes with man's innocent enjoyments. Sometimes they want to make us all into teetotallers, sometimes they

are out against boxing, or racing, or the stage ; sometimes they insist that we shall sit indoors all Sunday
afternoon and go to sleep. Wherever Protestant
opinion really rules a country, you always find legislation of one sort or another which is designed to stop
people being merry. It sounds distant and old-
fashioned to us, but that is because Protestantism has
lost its grip of the country. In the United States,
where the Protestants, though few in number, are rich
and powerful, the thing goes on to this day. And when
Protestantism does lose its grip, a reaction sets in, a
reaction against Puritanism, which instead of making
people merry makes them dissolute. A false religion,
no less than lack of religion, will destroy, in the end, a
nation's peace of mind.

Let us comfort ourselves, then, those of us who love
England, with the thought that in trying to convert
England we are not trying to alter her into something
that is strange and foreign : we are trying to make her
once more merry England—that which she was and
that which traditionally she ought to be. Those who
hate our religion are fond of pointing us to the example
of Catholic nations abroad, of which they draw a very
unfair picture, and then say : ' Look at Belgium—do
you want England to be like that ? Look at Spain—
do you want England to be like that ? ' But the
truth is that, for better or worse, England will never
be quite like any other country. You may love her,
you may hate her, but you must take her as she
stands. Those native virtues that now grow wild in
her hedgerows will only bloom the stronger and the
fairer when the faith cultivates them. The more
England becomes Catholic, the more English she will
become.

Let us, then, on this feast of our patron, pray
earnestly and resolve always to pray earnestly for the

conversion of the country we love. Let us ask his prayers, and the prayers of our Blessed Lady and the English martyrs, that the tide of conversions we see chronicled year by year may flow still more strong, and still more deep, till at last the heart of the country reawakes, and remembers, and returns to her ancient love. It will hardly be in our time, I suppose, that the change comes ; but even now we can stand, like Moses on Mount Nebo, and see beneath us the promised land that is one day to be our Catholic heritage. Let us stand together, strong in the faith of that vision, and resolve that through no fault of ours, no lapse of ours, no neglect of ours, that high endeavour to which we are pledged shall fall short of a swift and a lasting achievement. May the prayers of St. George protect this country that is dedicated to his honour, and bring all those who do him honour to that true country of ours which is in heaven.

III. ST. GREGORY THE GREAT

(Preached to schoolboys at St. Edmund's, Ware.)

Now therefore you are no more strangers and foreigners, but you are fellow citizens with the Saints. *Ephesians* ii, 19.

I DO not know if we always pay quite enough attention, except, of course, for the really big days, to the Saints whose feasts come round year by year. The smaller ones are apt to pass altogether unnoticed, and even the bigger ones come suddenly and take us by surprise. The Saint I want to speak of now is to-day's Saint, whose name, in case you did not catch it when the Collect was sung, is St. Gregory—St. Gregory the Great.

His name is derived from *egregora*, which, as the prefects would tell you, is the strong perfect (with Attic reduplication) of the Greek verb *egeiro*, to wake up. So St. Gregory is the wide-awake man, the man who is always on the spot ; there are no flies on him, as the Americans say. I suppose the Church has seldom had a ruler who got through more business. He wrote enormous quantities of theology, and is counted as one of the four great Latin doctors—you will see him pushing our Lord's chariot in the picture in the *ambulacrum*. He was one of the great early legislators of the Church, especially in matters of liturgy. And all the time, a profound statesman, he was guiding the destinies of the Church through a most difficult period of history, thinking nothing too insignificant or too remote for his personal attention. And one of the very remote and insignificant things he organized was the conversion of an island somewhere off the coast of France, called Britain. The Britons, in the classical authors, are always used as a synonym for the extreme limit, the outside edge of mankind—those Britons, tucked away right at the end of the world, much as we should say ' Borneo ' or ' Patagonia.' And I should think in St. Gregory's time, owing to the invasion of the Angles and Saxons, England was a still more inaccessible and unheard-of region. And that is where St. Gregory sent St. Augustine to convert you and me when we were little heathens.

Let us tell ourselves the story again, as the Venerable Bede tells it us, and all the history books tell it in imitation of him. Just imagine that you are an English boy, who went to the seaside and stayed on paddling when his mother told him not to, and a lot of disreputable Danes, coming back from a marauding expedition, bundled you, a whole lot of you, on board their ship and sold you at the nearest French port for the price of a drink. And then you have drifted about from one slave-dealer to another all over Europe, and finally you are standing about in a large market-place at Rome, in the very centre of the world. You are looking bored and sulky, and there is a placard over your head to say : ' This size £12.' And then a stranger comes up, and says something to the slave-dealer, obviously something like : ' Poor kids ! ' A very kind-looking gentleman this, all dressed in a long black gown. And he asks who you are, and the man says : ' Angles,' and you expect the same old joke you've heard all over Europe, about your looking rather obtuse Angles, but no ! it doesn't come. It's quite a new one this time. ' Angles ! You mean Angels ? That's the right name for them ; at least, they look like Angels, and it's a pity they are not fellow-citizens of the Angels in heaven. What part of Anglia do they come from ? ' ' Oh, from Deiri.' ' Well, they ought to be saved *de ira Dei* '—you probably will not understand that joke, since it is in Latin, but the bystanders seem to find it very funny. ' And what is their king called ? ' The kind gentleman does not have quite such luck this time ; their king is called Aella. However, he does his best, and says something about what a good thing it would be if Aella's subjects learned to sing Alleluia. And they all laugh again ; only the kind gentleman goes on his way looking rather serious.

Well, of course, the kind gentleman was St. Gregory. He was a very holy man, but he did not mind making jokes ; there is hope in that for all of us. And he was a very clever man, but he did not mind making rather bad jokes ; there is hope in that for some of us. I am afraid, though, that the details of that story are not quite certain. St. Bede simply hands it on as a tradition he has heard ; and the earliest form of the story does not make the Angles slaves or boys at all ; just grown-up Angles who happened to be visiting Rome. And with that, of course, all the point of their looking like Angels is lost. We think of the slave-boys looking very good and clean, like those cherubs with red cheeks and tow-coloured hair on the Christmas cards. I daresay really English boys, even then, would have looked rather grubby little brutes, and no one would have mistaken them for Angels. But the real point, you know, is quite unaffected by what they looked like. The real point is that they were citizens of Anglia, and St. Gregory said they ought to be fellow-citizens of the Angels. That was just like St. Gregory, and the age of St. Gregory. He objected to their Angularity. The Church had just begun to realize that she was outliving the Roman Empire, and saw in the spreading of the faith not a philosophy to be preached to the world, but a citizenship to be extended to it. It had been the boast of the Roman Empire that it made the most distant and most barbarous tribes into citizens of a single world-state :

She (prouder boast than other conquerors knew)
Gently the captives to her bosom drew ;
Mother, not mistress, made the thrall her kin,
And 'neath her wing drew all the nations in.
Orontes knows in Syria, Rhone in Gaul,
One speech, one race, one governance for all :
Whate'er is Earth, is Rome ; Rome stands till Earth
    shall fall.

St. Gregory, then, like the statesman he was, thinks of these Anglians not as ignorant people who need to be instructed, but as unhappy barbarians whose hearts must be conquered in order that a citizenship may be extended to them—the citizenship of the Angelic kingdom.

When we received the faith, we received it not (as other nations) like a microbe which we caught from our neighbours, nor as a bargain which we picked up from travelling pedlars, we were simply annexed to Rome by a single act of spiritual conquest. I do not say that there were not Christians wandering about in England before St. Augustine came. I do not say that the Irish would not have converted us sooner or later even if the Italians had not been first. All I say is that as a matter of fact our conversion was a purely Roman affair. You will still, occasionally, read of Protestant fellow-countrymen of ours referring to the Catholic Church in England under the contemptuous title of ' the Italian Mission.' The name is meant, of course, to twit us with being foreigners, because during the penal times our priests were educated abroad. It is a delightful idea : you make the Mass high treason, and put a price on every priest's head, and so seminaries have to be built abroad, and priests have to come back from foreign centres if they want to preserve the old faith. And when they do come back, you greet them with shouts of : ' Oh, you beastly Italian.' Well, I am not considering here whether that is a very generous taunt, or a very intelligent one : the interesting point about it is, Who was the first to make it ? It was made first by Archbishop Benson, father of Mgr Hugh Benson. And what was he ? Archbishop of Canterbury. And why Canterbury ? Why that very one-horse, dead-and-alive place on the South-Eastern ? Simply because St. Augustine, not being able to go on as far as London, had to wait about there for a time and so set up his See there. St. Augustine, a Roman envoy sent by the Pope to convert our country to the religion of the Church of Rome. And then an Archbishop of Canterbury describes the diocese of Westminster as an Italian Mission !

Well, we were founded from Rome ; and all through the Middle Ages, in spite of the nuisance of living so far away from it, we were known for our loyalty to the Roman See. In St. Gregory's time men were looking to the Church as the one abiding institution ; it seemed to them that the break-up of earthly dominions and the shifting of nations which was taking place throughout Europe pointed to mere chaos ahead, unless hope lay in the Papacy. To-day there is the same break-up of great dominions ; the same shifting of the limits of nationality. The world has altered its look. since we learned our geography, and it has not got to the end of its alteration yet. In this new world men still look to the Catholic Church, and to Rome as the divinely-appointed centre of the Catholic Church, as the one abiding institution which will survive the new chaos. And we, without ceasing to be Angles (those of us who are Angles), will have to rally more than ever round the Holy See as the centre of our true citizenship, that Angelic citizenship which was St. Gregory's gift to us. We ought to be praying earnestly for the Holy Father. We ought to be praying for the conversion of those who, disheartened by the failure of civilization, are turning to the Church for guidance.

May the King of Angels bring us all to the fellowship of the heavenly citizens ; to him be glory for ever and ever. Amen.

IV. ST. EDWARD THE CONFESSOR

(Preached at St. Edwards, Golders Green.)

For the hope of the wicked is as dust which is blown away with the wind, and as a thin froth which is dispersed by the storm, and a smoke that is scattered abroad by the wind, and as the remembrance of a guest of one day that passeth by. But the just shall live for evermore, and their reward is with the Lord, and the care of them with the most High. *Wisdom* v, 15.

SOMETHING like two months back there died, with the greatest publicity that can attend a death-bed, one of the most characteristic and one of the most successful figures of our time. A man of business, he had restricted himself to a single form of business— that journalism which sells to the public the news it wants to hear told and the views it wants to hear expressed. A man of political ambition, he contented himself with a single form of political activity—that journalism which praises or blames, and to the best of its power appoints or dismisses, parliaments and ministers of the Crown. Hewing his own way up the difficult path of public fame by the force of his native energy, he achieved a position of prominence almost unrivalled in our memory. True, it was not one of personal prominence; we did not often see his portrait or hear what manner of man he was : many whose thought he influenced from day to day did not even know his title. True again, it was a precarious power he exercised; for the newspaper proprietor, while he aspires to be the tyrant of public opinion, must in many ways stoop to be its slave. Yet within those limits he stood before the world a titanic figure ; and when a banquet was given in his honour, a clergyman of the Established Church tactfully included his name among the blessings which he commemorated at grace. Did he do good in the world, or evil ? Probably a good deal of both, and both alike accident- ally, for he had no mission to preach, and no selfish cupidity to satisfy. Only one thing he asked, the power of an enormous publicity, and that wish was granted him : never, probably, has a man succeeded so utterly in that which he set before himself to accom- plish. And then God required his soul of him, and he died.

He died, and they held a memorial service for him. They held a memorial service for him in Westminster Abbey, that strange mausoleum of nine hundred years of English history which is neither church nor cathedral, because it is too proud to be either. And as the great congregation that celebrated his obsequies reminded one another, to the plaintive pealing of the organ, that

Time like an ever-rolling stream bears all its sons away ;
They fly forgotten, as a dream dies at the opening day,

how many of them gave a thought to the poignantly contrasted character of that English king who built the Abbey, and who still keeps in the Abbey his unhonoured shrine ? That king, whose more than royal memory the universal Church celebrates at this time ?

Let me give you in brief *his* biography. Born to a throne bequeathed to him by a line of strong men, whose vigorous qualities he was little likely to emulate, he was driven into exile at the age of ten years ; it seemed that a fortunate catastrophe had robbed him of the terrors of royalty. Himself, patient under that exile, he declared that he would rather remain uncrowned than win a kingdom at the cost of blood.

That hope was unrealized ; he was restored with the goodwill of the Norman Duke, already England's rival and soon to be her invader. Very naturally, he took for his advisers and administrators men of the race that had befriended his exile. Insignificant in person (he was probably an albino) and lacking at least in his public policy the sterner qualities of mind, he became a puppet king in the hands of an unpopular clique, his mother's kinsmen. There was a revolt, and his Norman advisers fled the country ; he became a puppet king once more, overshadowed this time by the figure of the great Saxon earl whose daughter he had taken to wife. Taken, rather, for his spouse : for they had no children, and it is constantly asserted that they never lived as man and wife. The one benefit he might have conferred upon his country, by leaving an heir in whose veins Norman and Saxon blood would mingle, he refused of his own choice. His kingdom, already pledged to the Normans, he now had to bequeath to a Saxon champion. Foreseeing clearly in his last moments the harvest of slaughter which was to be the reaping of his own peaceful reign, he died. He died, and thirty-six years later they found his body uncorrupted, and breathing the odour of sanctity.

What a record of failure ! What a negation of all that the politicians value, and all that the historians revere ! Other Saints, other kings whose memory is venerated, have been no less ineffective in their lives, yet breathe some atmosphere of tragedy which endeared them to posterity. St. Peter Celestine was unequal to the task of government, but he signalized himself in history by resigning the triple tiara. Henry of Windsor was a weak man born in a distracted age, but the story of his murder rallied to him the sympathies of his people. Edward, no less incompetent in his lifetime than St. Peter Celestine or the sixth Henry,

died crowned and died a natural death. One great
thing he gave to his country, the Abbey Church of
Westminster. And that church, with an absence of
humour singular even among our fellow-countrymen,
they have chosen to be the burial-place of England's
great national heroes—not asking what creed they held
or what life they lived, but only whether they achieved
fame.

> Mortality, behold and Fear !
> What a change of flesh is here !
> Here they lie had realms and lands,
> Who now want strength to stir their hands,
> Where, from their pulpits sealed with dust,
> They preach, ' in greatness is no trust.'
> Here's an acre sown indeed
> With the richest, royallest seed
> That the earth did e'er suck in
> Since the first man died for sin.

Soldier, and statesman, and lawyer, they wait for
the last trumpet, and the world's dissolution, and the
great Assize. And amidst them all sleeps the poor
weakling who graced so ill the throne of England,
and they are stared at by visitors, while he, the builder
of the Abbey, is forgotten.

We know that there is another side to the picture, a
side to which historians, full of great world movements
and the fortunes of dynasties, pay scant attention. We
know that if he abstained from the use of marriage it
was because he hoped to win the palm of virginity.
We know that while Norman duke and Saxon earl
forgot the poor puppet who had served their turn and
slipped through their hands, the poor, better canonizers
than earl or duke, remembered the good king Edward
as the man who had remitted their taxes and lavished
his own fortune upon their needs. We know that in
his lifetime men loved him for his gentleness and kind-

ness of heart, and that both in life and death Almighty
God ratified their judgement by granting him miraculous favours. But for all his practical effect upon
our history he might as well never have lived, had
better, perhaps, never have reigned. When we venerate
St. Edward, we venerate a failure.

We do so advisedly. Not because success in life
necessarily falls to the grasping and the unscrupulous,
so that success itself should be mistrusted by Christians
as a sign of rascality. Not that there have not been
great Saints who were also great kings, great statesmen, great warriors, St. Oswald, St. Dunstan, St.
Joan of Arc. But because we will not let ourselves be
blinded by the lure of worldly success so as to forget
that the true statesmanship is exercised in the council
chamber, and the true warfare fought on the battle-
field of the human soul. Ask yourself which you
would rather have been, in life, of all those great dead
who lie in Westminster Abbey, and you will find it a
difficult question to answer : there is so much that
dazzles, so much that captivates the imagination.
Would you rather have written this, have painted
that, have built that, have discovered that, have won
this triumph or have carried that enactment—you can
hardly say. But ask yourself which of those great dead
you would rather be now, your body there, your soul
far away—is there any Christian who would not ask
to change places with the Confessor ; who would not
choose his resting-place, there to wait for the opening
of the great Doomsday Book, in which nothing is
recorded of men, but whether they meant good or
evil, whether they loved or neglected God ?

The hope of the wicked is as dust which is blown
away . . . but the reward of the just is for evermore.
All through this very beautiful passage in the Book of
Wisdom the just man is the simpleton, the natural

prey of designing enemies. They deride him, they make him a parable of reproach ; they esteem his life madness and his end without honour. All the maxims of worldly prudence, all the sensible considerations, seem to be on their side. The best that can happen to him, the just man, is that he should be taken away, lest wickedness should alter his understanding, or deceit beguile his soul. He is not fit to fight the cunning of his age with its own weapons. And, by a defiant paradox, the book is called the Book of Wisdom! It is a deliberate paradox, for the word ' wise ' in Scriptural language has often the sense of crafty ; the Unjust Steward is commended because he acted wisely, and the children of this world in their generation are wiser than the children of light. But there is a wisdom which somehow these innocent, gullible, ineffective, open-handed simpletons have got hold of, while these smart, up-to-date, very much alive men of business have missed it. Now, which is right ?

Our Divine Lord, quoting from the Psalms of David, has assured us that the meek shall possess the earth. Does that mean that meekness is one of those qualities which will gain men a brighter crown in the heavenly kingdom that is to come ? It does, of course, but does it mean nothing more ? Certainly in this, as in any other age of history, it does not seem as if it is the meek who carry off the world's prizes ; go where you will, the advertisements of the mind-training systems and the correspondence colleges will cry out to you that life is a stern battle, that success is for the ambitious, and that the weakest goes to the wall. There is no room, it would seem, for the saintly albinos. Does Christianity, then, simply preach the survival of the unfittest, by promising us in heaven a reversal of all human values and a revision of all human judgements ? And must it always be, in this world, the Godwins and the Harolds and the Williams who have the best time, make the best use of their opportunities ?

The land of a certain rich man brought forth plenty of fruits. And he thought within himself, saying : What shall I do, because I have no room here to bestow my fruits? And he said : This will I do ; I will pull down my barns, and will build greater, and into them I will gather all things that are grown to me and my goods. And I will say to my soul : Soul, thou hast much goods laid up for many years : take thy rest, eat, drink, make good cheer. But God said to him : Thou fool, this night do they require thy soul of thee. And whose shall those things be which thou hast provided ? So is he that layeth up treasure for himself and is not rich towards God. In that telling, almost bitter parable, Our Divine Lord has shown us the fallacy of the successful life, not only from the point of view of the next world, but even in this. If the rich fool had not died then, do you think he would really have carried out his resolution of retiring from business ? Not he. He would have gone on, as he had already gone on all those years, wearing himself out in the pursuit of a visionary contentment which he continually promised himself, yet could never rest to enjoy it. A record harvest ? Why, then, he must build yet greater barns. And when the barns were built, he would have extended his farming operations so as to have more fruits to fill them with. He was a fool, because he became the slave of his own ambitions. Mind you, we are not told that he was wicked. We are not told that, like Dives, he neglected the poor, and went like Dives into the place of torment. No, we are only told that he was a fool ; that his life was a wasted one. No doubt but his funeral sermon and his obituary notices called him a successful man ; a pioneer of agriculture, and one who had

revolutionized the old type of barn. But in the stillness
of the night in which God spoke to him, he knew that
he was a failure.

His was a selfish life ; not all the lives the world calls
successful are selfish lives. Many of those who sleep in
King Edward's Abbey were devoted servants of their
kind, who left the world better for their passing. But
this is certain, that true satisfaction came to them and
true success crowned them only so far as their ambitions
were for a cause, not for a party, for others, not for
themselves. Man's happiness lies in devoting himself,
his success in the offering he can make. And our
Confessor was a successful man, yes, even in this
world, because in his simple piety, in the unaffected
generosity of his nature, he set himself to serve men
about him by easing their burdens, by relieving their
necessities, by confirming them in their allegiance to
the faith. Great opportunities passed him by, and he
never marked them ; he might have altered the
dynastic history of England, have left us different
manners and a different political constitution, if he
had been other than he was. Instead, he left all these
things to God's Providence ; and God's Providence,
using the ambitions of human agents as its puppets,
moulded our history beyond man's expectation. And
what do they mean to us now, those human agents ?
Mere names in the history book, mere stiff, attitudiniz-
ing figures on the Bayeux Tapestry, they have become
part of a past hardly less remote to us than legend.
As dust which is blown away with the wind, and as a
thin froth that is dispersed by the storm, and a smoke
that is scattered abroad by the wind, and as the
remembrance of a guest of one day that passeth by.
The Conqueror, who diverted the stream of history,
went to his grave disappointed and lies there a historical memory. The Confessor, whose ambitions

could be satisfied by finding a poor man his dinner, saw no corruption in death, and lives, the patron of his fellow-countrymen.

One only task he set before himself that had any external magnificence about it, and that was characteristic of him. It was no fortress, no royal palace, no court of justice that he planned : the House of God lay waste, and he must rebuild it. And, as if it were a symbol of the life he lived, built together from little acts of kindness and little sacrifices of self, stone by stone and arch by arch rose the Abbey Church of Westminster, which for all the additions and the restorations 'that have altered it in the course of the centuries, we still call his church. The building was actually completed about a week before his death : and, if pride held any place in his gentle character, he must have felt proud to think that he had left one lasting memorial ; that while his monks continued their daily round of prayer, the last of the dynasty of Egbert would not be forgotten.

And yet, though his Abbey still stands, and even his shrine was protected—ironically enough, by the shadow of royalty—from desecration, the liturgy of the Church he loved so well is no more celebrated in the house he built for it. Westminster, with all the other monuments of our Catholic antiquity, has passed into other hands and hears strange doctrines preached. It has remained for devoted men in the last two generations to replace, as best they could with the resources they had at their disposal, that loss suffered by religion. And among the churches that have thus been raised, not the least remarkable for its splendid proportions and its commanding site is this church in which we claim his patronage to-day. And this church, too, will perpetuate the memory of a founder, in whom those who knew him at all could not but discern the signs of a saintly character. Here was another unsuccessful life, as the world judges success— a life in which a spirit of indomitable energy was long thwarted in its activities and too soon cut off by a discipline of terrible and (the world would say) meaningless suffering. You have done well to commemorate him at its high altar ; for its history is bound up with his ; and so long as the Holy Sacrifice is offered in this place, it should be offered with grateful memory of the prayers and the cruel mortifications which Father Bendon used to offer for his parish and his people.

Their reward is with the Lord, and the care of them with the most High. May the prayers of Our Blessed Lady, and St. Edward our patron, and all the Saints of God bring us safely from this world of humiliation and of suffering into the kingdom of the just.

V. ST. ANSELM

(Preached at St. Anselm and St. Cecilia's, Kingsway.)

And I said : Woe is me, because I have held my peace, because I am a man of unclean lips, and I dwell in the midst of a people that hath unclean lips, and I have seen with my eyes the King, the Lord of hosts. *Isaias* vi, 5.

IT is a curious thing what a lot of coincidences there are in history. Three Archbishops of Canterbury, and only three, between the Norman Conquest and the time of England's apostasy, have been raised to the altars of the Church ; St. Thomas, the patron of all our secular clergy, your patron St. Anselm, and my

patron St. Edmund. Each of those three men spent a
significant part of his time of office in exile overseas.
They belonged, respectively, to the reigns of Henry I,
Henry II, and Henry III. The attitude of the reigning
sovereign was, in each case, the cause of the Saint's
difficulties and of his consequent merits—a gloomy
omen for the day when an eighth Henry should arise,
and a time-server be found enthroned at Lambeth.

And there is a singular sort of mathematical pro-
gression, I think, about the three characters if you
consider them side by side. St. Edmund was made
Archbishop because he was a Saint and everybody
knew it. St. Thomas was made Archbishop because
he was the last person you would have expected to
become a Saint—you might almost as well have
expected it of Thomas Cromwell, or of Thomas
Cranmer. St. Edmund's temperament produces few
Archbishops but many Saints, St. Thomas' few Saints
but many Archbishops. St. Edmund would have been
a far happier man if he had never worn a mitre ; his
archbishopric was only an addition to his long series of
mortifications. St. Thomas, humanly speaking, only
learned to develop his Sainthood as the result of being
made Archbishop ; his archbishopric was the occasion
of his self-realization. St. Edmund was a Saint first
and an Archbishop afterwards ; he learned to be great
in spite of being good. With St. Thomas, in order of
time, the process was reversed ; he learned to be good
in spite of being great. To put it roughly, and merely
from the human point of view, you may say that St.
Edmund probably would not have become Archbishop
if he had not been a Saint, and St. Thomas would not
have become a Saint if he had not been Archbishop.

In your holy patron St. Anselm these opposing
characteristics are curiously reconciled. When he first
set foot in our country you may say that he already

had all St. Edmund's qualifications for heaven, and all St. Thomas' qualifications for Lambeth. Take away his prelacy, and you still leave a character comparable with that of St. Edward the Confessor. Take away his saintliness, and you still leave a career that rivals the career of Lanfranc. This was the man who, with some misgiving, came over to visit a sick friend in England at a time when the archbishopric of Canterbury had long been left vacant, so that King William Rufus and his creatures might enjoy the sequestrated revenues of the See. You will read in Dean Church's life of St. Anselm how at Christmas, 1092, the clergy were allowed to pray for a remedy for the misfortunes of the Church. You will read on the next page how, early in 1093 (which means, if you come to think of it, about a fortnight later) King William fell sick and was evidently at the point of death. The Anglican biographer does not seem to connect the two events even by way of coincidence : fortunately for himself, the Norman king was more prompt in seeing the point of the situation. He promised amendment and restitution of every possible kind, and sent for Anselm at once as the obvious person to be elected Archbishop.

And then began a scene which has been enacted with various results a thousand times in the history of sanctity, but seldom with so much publicity or so much dramatic interest as in St. Anselm's case. When you try to make a Saint accept a bishopric, it is like trying to make a child take medicine : the result is a perfect fury of dissent. Calculation, argument, even personal dignity are thrown to the winds ; the Saint like the child simply sticks to his point and says : ' I won't, I won't, I won't.' In this case not merely the ordinary considerations but the whole welfare of a long-widowed Church and, as seemed probable, the life of a notorious sinner were depending upon St. Anselm's acceptance,

and he simply refused. ' A great post like the archbishopric,' writes Dean Church, ' may have had
irresistible terrors, overwhelming all its attractions or
temptations, to a religious mind and conscience in the
eleventh century '—a comment that speaks better for
the courage of eleventh-century bishops than for the
sense of humour of nineteenth-century deans. Anyhow, it was only by the use of physical force that they
dragged the Saint to the King's bedside ; and there,
pressing the crozier against the knuckles that would
not open so as to hold it, they elected the Archbishop
of Canterbury.

St. Anselm is, from many points of view, a famous
man, and stood out like a giant among his contemporaries. Yet the work he did was not final, for no
human work is final. He was a monastic reformer, but
others carried monastic reform further after his death.
He was an intrepid champion of the Church against
the Crown ; and that is the same thing as to say that
he defended the prerogatives of St. Peter with a firm-
ness which no glosses of the historian can conceal :
but even here his work had to be done over again by
St. Thomas à Becket. He was a philosopher and a
theologian, yet to-day his theological views are generally quoted in order to be refuted, and his most famous
exploit in philosophy, the ontological proof of the
existence of God, is not only discredited but has,
according to some, the dubious credit of being the
parent of modern idealism. So I will not apologize for
leaving out these considerations—the sort of considerations you get in an obituary notice—and asking you
to concentrate your attention on the scene I was
describing just now, and to consider with me why it
was that the Saints, why it was that St. Anselm, always
began by refusing, and sometimes succeeded in refusing altogether, the offer of ecclesiastical preferment ?

Was it because the Saints were incompetent in the managing of affairs, and knew it ? That might have been true in some cases, but it certainly was not in St. Anselm's ; he had already given good proof of his competency by being Abbot of a large monastery—running a monastery is not always a sinecure. Or was it that they thought they were incompetent although they were not ? Surely, if that had been all, obedience should have triumphed over humility, and they should have been content to acquiesce in the estimate others had formed of their worth. Or were they simply afraid that they would not get enough time to say their prayers ? But St. Anselm was a very busy man already. Or were they afraid of the temptation to worldliness, to love of money, to subservience which high office brings with it ? But they must have known that other candidates were, humanly speaking, much more likely to succumb to those temptations than themselves : the good man, Plato tells us, accepts office in the State not for any advantage he gets from it, but because he fears the possibility of worse men than himself attaining to office instead. Or was it that they disliked all the pomp and fuss of it ? But they could keep their secret intention pure. All those ordinary reasons which would make it very bad for you or me to be made a bishop were alleged by the Saints as excuses, but surely only as excuses. There must be some deeper reason to explain this phenomenon that is always meeting us in hagiography, from St. Celestine resigning the triple tiara to the Curé d'Ars running away like a schoolboy from the little French parish where everybody idolized him.

It is not that the Saint has become unpractical, like the philosopher : the philosopher blinks because he has come out of the darkness of his study into the light of common things ; the Saint blinks because he has come out of the light of his oratory into the darkness of the world. He has been with God ; and in seeing, as we do not see, the greatness of God, he has seen, as we do not see, his own smallness. It is not that he exaggerates his smallness ; he is not like the horse, which shies (so clever people tell us) because its eyes are focused wrong and it sees everything around it twice as big as it really is. No, the Saint has got the true perspective, and we the false. Woe is me, because I have held my peace—in the solitude of prayer he has learned his own miserable helplessness. I am a man of unclean lips, and dwell in the midst of a people of unclean lips—he has no illusion, you see, about his neighbours being to any great extent better than himself. And I have seen with my eyes the King, the Lord of Hosts—that is it. To the man who has once seen himself as he looks in comparison with God, all worldly preferment, not because it is too high or because it is too low a sphere for his attainments, not because others seem more competent to fill the post, not because it entails labour or responsibility, but simply because it must in some measure make him the recipient of worldly homage and give him honour in the sight of men, is an anomaly not to be thought of, a miscarriage of justice to be avoided at all costs.

It is not a question of one man being more or being less worthy than another, the plain fact is, if you have only got your eyes focused right, that any job is too big for any of us, because all worldly station involves the bestowing of some credit, and bestowing it where in truth credit is not due. Modesty is quite a different thing from humility. It is a very attractive thing, modesty, even where it is something of an affectation. The boy, for example, who got the D.S.O. almost immediately after leaving school, and when we asked him what he was doing when he got it could only reply : ' Oh, I don't know, fooling round somewhere, I suppose '—that is modesty. There is a great deal of modesty going about ; it is fashionable, and the lack of it stamps you with vulgarity—a lot of modesty, but very little humility. For modesty is only the disinclination to hear our own praises sounded above those of other men ; by humility man learns that simply because he is man he is nothing. Of such humility the Queen of Heaven herself could leave us an example ; let us make it the subject of our prayer on St. Anselm's festival. We can find excuses for ourselves when we do not rival the Saints in their heroic exercise of other virtues, but it is not so with their humility. For in proportion as we are less than they, with all the more justice can it be claimed of us that we should be humble.

And remember, this Christian humility does not unfit a man for great deeds. A critic of St. Edmund might say of his *Nolo episcopari* : ' Well, perhaps after all he was right ; perhaps a more unscrupulous man would have made a more successful job of the archbishopric in his day.' But St. Anselm does not even leave room for the worldly point of view. He knew, in his humility, that neither he nor any other man living was worthy of the crozier that was pressed against his clenched fingers, but, once clasped, it was clasped in a grip of iron. We must not be afraid, then, of the meditation of our own littleness : it could not dim the lustre of Anselm's earthly fame, yet made his coronal in heaven shine, who knows how much brighter ? May his prayers protect the Church he laboured in life to defend, still bringing back stubborn hearts to the allegiance of the Holy See : his prayers win for each one of us the grace he most needs, to God's glory and our eternal salvation.

VI. ST. DOMINIC

(Preached at St. Dominic's, Haverstock Hill.)

Ye are the salt of the earth. But if the salt lose its savour, wherewith shall it be salted ? *Matthew* v, 13.

TWO men, at the beginning of the thirteenth century, were raised up by God to season his Church, that seemed in danger of perishing through its own corruption. They were both comparatively short-lived. God will be glorified, now in a short life-time, now in the fullness of years ; St. John Vianney, whom we celebrate on Thursday, died worn out with his labours at the age of seventy-three ; St. Laurence, whom we celebrate on Friday, was cut down by per-secution during his diaconate. If you add the ages of St. Francis and St. Dominic together, they do not cover a full century. And the career of St. Dominic is particularly remarkable, because he did not find out what his life's work was to be until he was thirty-five years old, with only sixteen more years to live. That short time sufficed for doing the special thing God had called him to do ; for meeting a particular situation, and warding off a particular danger from the gates of Christendom. If you will bear with me, I will sketch very briefly—at the risk of repeating things you may have heard yesterday and the day before—what that situation, what that danger was.

Two important heresies at that time threatened the peace, and perhaps the life of the Church ; the Waldensian and the Albigensian heresies. The Wal-denses, of whom a remnant still remains in Italy, seem to have been among the most harmless of the sects ;

erring through their simpleness rather than through any constructive malice. Scandalized by the riches of the higher clergy, by the sight of so many priests living unpriestly lives, they formed themselves into a little Protestant community before the time of Protestantism was yet come. They lived in poverty, they studied and translated the Bible, they refused, like the Anabaptists and the Quakers after them, to bind themselves by any form of oath. Their main false doctrine was that a priest living in mortal sin was no priest at all ; and they thought to replace the ministry of the ordained clergy by a kind of lay ministry of their own. They were, if such a phrase may be used, Noncomformists rather than heretics ; and it is possible that, if they had not been involved in the fate of less worthy neighbours, they would have been treated by the Church with leniency, and returned gradually to her communion.

But the Albigenses, who resembled them outwardly, because they too made a parade of great simplicity and innocence, were the revival or the continuation of a very old and very dangerous heresy ; that Manichean heresy which attracted, for a time, the restless genius of St. Augustine. In order to account for the existence of the evil in the world, the Manichean maintains a total divorce between matter and spirit, believing that matter is of its nature evil, and owes its existence not to the Providence of God but to the interference of a malign spirit. Accordingly, he rejects the doctrine of the Incarnation, which degrades, to his mind, the spiritual nature of the Godhead. The more fully initiated of the sect, who called themselves the Perfect, repudiated altogether the use of marriage, and abstained, in their diet, from all animal life and whatever owed its origin to animal life. They were the declared enemies of Christendom, and, patronized as

they were by the Count of Toulouse, threatened to
supersede it altogether in the southern districts of
France.

We remember St. Dominic and his order, in the first
instance, for the intellectual protest which they opposed
to that sinister outbreak of Oriental philosophy in the
heart of Western Christendom. Heresies, after all, have
their place in the elucidation of religious truth. The
fine flower of Christian scholarship is fertilized, you
may say, by the decaying corpse of false doctrine. Or
perhaps you may say with greater accuracy that
Christian theology has at all times been a reaction to
the assaults of heresy, just as a living organism will
develop a protective shell there, where a hostile
stimulus from without has made itself felt. When the
germs of the Manichean heresy sought to find a lodge-
ment in the healthy body of Christendom, the reaction
of that healthy body was the great Dominican tradition
of learning. It developed, we may well believe,
beyond the Saint's own hope. Almost at the moment
of his death another Saint was being born to carry on
his work ; St. Thomas, destined like Eliseus to have a
double portion of his Master's spirit. Who shall say
what we owe to that Providential impetus which the
Manichean peril gave to Christian thought ? Just as
a healthy body may gain immunity from a disease by
being inoculated with a mild form of it, so Christian
thought was immunized against the false doctrines
which threatened to destroy it, three centuries later,
by its inoculation with the dying germs of Orientalism
which it had encountered, and triumphed over, at
Toulouse.

That intellectual protest we associate especially with
the Dominican order, because it is more individually,
more characteristically theirs. The sons of St. Francis
only entered the vineyard of scholarship as late-

comers, by a happy deflection from their original design. But meanwhile, let us not forget that the coming of the Friars was a moral protest too ; and in that moral protest the sons of St. Dominic from the first took, and were meant to take, their full part ; Cherubim and Seraphim must hymn together the dazzling holiness of God. Those were times, it is sad to say it, in which the Church seemed to have lost the salt wherewith Christ had commissioned it to season the world. The great St. Bernard was dead ; and the monastic orders, even at their best, were too remote from the world to affect powerfully the standard of Christian living. There were crying abuses ; and, whereas the Albigensians, a purely destructive movement, deserve little of our sympathy, the poor Waldenses could at least claim that they had reason for the disaffection which made them the antagonists of the Church. An intellectual heresy can be met by the weapons of the intellect ; a moral protest, such as that of the Waldenses, can only be met by a rival moral protest within the Church itself. Just as the tide of the Reformation was stemmed, not merely by polemical writing and preaching, but by the great spiritual renewal which was accomplished throughout Europe by the Saints of the sixteenth century, so three hundred years earlier it was not only the learning of the Friars, but their poverty, their chastity, the simplicity of their lives and manners, that saved Europe for the faith.

Reverend Fathers, the times in which we live, seven hundred years removed from those days of persecution and terror, still need the intellectual protest, still need the moral. The old difficulty of reconciling God's omnipotence with his benevolence still presses upon us ; and to-day, instead of trying to save the one at the expense of the other, like the medieval heretics, men are driven, by that apparent inconsistency, to deny his very existence. It is to you, with the old weapons in your hands, that we look for the solving of these difficulties as of those ; like King David, when he found once more the sword with which he slew the giant in the valley of the terebinth, ' there is none like that' we say, ' give it me.' But while we call upon you as scholars for an intellectual protest against the tendencies of the age, we call upon you as Friars for a moral protest as well. For the times are evil ; and the world's mind would not have travelled so far from God if its heart had not travelled far from God first.

We heard much lately in the newspapers—not so much quite lately, for the newspapers tire of their fancies quickly—about a new religious movement in the Protestant world around us which was to have prodigious effects in bringing men back to the service of God. It has much in common with earlier revivalist movements ; and in one point at least it may well remind us of the Waldenses, about whom we were speaking just now. The Waldenses, as I was saying, distrusted the ministrations of an ordained clergy ; every good man, they held, in so far as he is a good man, is a priest. Just so these new teachers have revived the idea of confession ; but their confessions are made, not to an ordained minister of whatever denomination, but to one another—to the friends in whose goodwill and spiritual insight they can trust. I do not know whether this particular movement is destined to fulfil the hopes of its promoters ; but of this at least I feel certain, that either this or some similar reaction will begin, before long, to stem the tide of demoralization which has so long closed in upon our society. Grace, like nature, abhors a vacuum ; and any public neglect of God and of the soul's needs will be followed, before long, by a return. Are we to suffer our fellow-countrymen to take refuge once more in the half-truths of a revived Protestantism, instead of learning to find peace where true peace can alone be found, in the bosom of the Catholic Church ?

We shall suffer them to do that, unless we can oppose to the revived spirit of Protestantism a revived spirit of Catholicism. We Catholics want more simplicity, more contentment with plain living and with common things, more unworldliness about money and social position, more daily trust in Providence, more honesty of speech, more kindliness towards our fellow-men ; we want to get away from a great deal of that complexity, that sophistication, that worship of good form, into which the influence of our modern surroundings has led us. We want to restore, somehow, not the outward conditions, but the moral attitude which belonged to the medieval world. It is to the mendicant orders, to you not less than to the Franciscans, that we must look if we are to revive that spirit of gaiety which goes with poverty, that open-hearted acceptance of the world which belongs only to those who have learned to despise it. Your continuous tradition must link us with our past, if we are to find refuge from this over-mechanized, over-commercialized age ; like a shaft bringing the fresh airs of the sea into a Tube station. Persuade us that the Catholic religion is something more than a mere label, a mere favour that a man can wear on his sleeve ; that it is a life, and an interpretation of life ; an attitude towards our daily tasks, as well as an attitude towards God.

We expect of you that to-day, as seven hundred years ago, you should leaven human thought, by justifying the ways of God to men ; by asserting the truth of our Lord's Incarnation, and vindicating the

honour of his Blessed Mother. We expect of you also
that to-day, as seven hundred years ago, you should
leaven human society, by showing us in your own lives,
and in the lives of that great Third Order which derives
its inspiration from you, the grand simplicity of former
times. So will men learn to find, in the Catholic
Church, the key to their disillusionment, and the
remedy for their despairs ; learning will not do that,
argument will not do that. May the prayers of your
holy patron, raised so long ago by an infallible oracle
to the altars of the Church, win such grace for you and
for us ; may the bewildered minds of our non-Catholic
fellow-countrymen be led back, more and more,
through the Dominicans to Dominic, and through
Dominic to Christ.

VII. ST. EDMUND OF ABINGDON

(Preached at St. Edmund's, Ware.)

And the priest said : Lo, here is the sword of Goliath the Philistine,
whom thou slewest in the valley of the terebinth. If thou wilt take
this, take it, for there is no other but this. And David said : There is
none like that ; give it me. I *Kings* xxi, 9.

WE have no means of knowing what was the age
of David when this interview took place. Certainly he was married, and had occupied an important
military position ; we may imagine him, perhaps, as
nearing thirty. The bitter jealousy of King Saul, the
master whom he had served so faithfully, had driven
him to take refuge as an outlaw among the hills. On
his way he visits the priests at Nobe, who supply him

and his followers with bread for their journey. Then
—it seems a poor chance, but he asks if they have a
sword there ; he has come out unarmed. And they
tell him : Yes, there is one sword, the sword of Goliath
the Philistine, the giant whom David himself slew,
and dedicated the sword he had plundered from his
body in the tabernacle of God.

As the priest is talking, David's mind travels back
over the years, ten years perhaps, and he sees the
valley of the terebinth as if it were yesterday. He sees
himself as a boy, rather tired and hot after his journey
from Bethlehem—he had been bringing presents from
his father to his three soldier brothers, a bushel of corn,
and ten loaves of bread, and ten small cheeses for their
commanding officer, with father's compliments. To
and fro along the valley strides the gigantic figure of
the Philistine, taunting the armies of Israel and chal-
lenging them to provide a champion who will meet
him in single combat. David remembers how he
expected his brothers to be pleased with their hamper
from home, and how disappointed he was at the very
elder-brotherly greeting of the eldest, Eliab : ' Why
camest thou hither ? And why didst thou leave those
few sheep in the desert ? I know thy pride, and the
wickedness of thy heart, that thou art come down to
see the battle.' So unfair of him—and besides, David
had wanted to see the battle rather. And then the
sudden resolve, to ask if he might accept the giant's
challenge—that heroic resolution, with just a faint
tinge of anxiety to get even with Eliab. It felt rather
frightening at first, walking down the valley to meet
the boaster—and then he was kneeling down by the
brook side, while he picked up five pebbles just the
shape he wanted ; and then the confidence he felt as
the sling whirled round his head, and the stone flew
dead straight, and hit his enemy full in the forehead,

so that he lay there stunned. Quick ! no time to be
lost ; weaponless himself, he takes out the giant's
sword and cuts off the monstrous head with it. And
then, a confused memory, the stir and the cry as the
men of Israel went out to battle. Yes, he has seen
many engagements since then ; many a sword has
broken in his victorious hand, but . . . the sword he
took from Goliath, what could bring better omens for
his present journey ? There is none like that ; give
it me !

Let me give you another picture for comparison—
one, perhaps, with which you are more familiar ;
St. Edmund on board ship, looking back at the cliffs
of Dover for the last time. He, too, is going into exile,
though it be voluntary exile ; he, too, is hated and
thwarted by the king for whom he has done so much,
for whom he would have done so much more. And
to him too, surely, comes a picture of the past ; only
he needs a longer retrospect ; it is nearly fifty years
now since he first made that Channel crossing. He
sees himself as a boy of fifteen or thereabouts, tre-
mendously excited at the prospect of going to study at
Paris. The sea itself was a stranger to him : he knew
the Thames where it sweeps down nobly from Oxford
to Abingdon, or where it hastens past the ferry at
Bablockhythe ; but the beauty and mystery of the
ships and the magic of the sea—that was all a new
experience. And probably, so wayward is memory in
the associations she brings together, he connects that
experience with the first time he wore a hair-shirt, his
mother's parting gift. Smile at the picture if you will,
but do not laugh at the symbol ; he was going to the
worldliest city of all time, and he was to keep himself
unspotted from the world. That love of Christ and his
Blessed Mother which he had learned at Oxford were
to be put to a severer test now. Since then, St.

Edmund has met the world at a hundred different
angles in the course of his busy life, has done heroic
penance, has inflicted cruel mortification on himself.
But those first impressions of his boyhood, which the
hair-shirt symbolizes, are still his formative impressions ; the religion of his boyhood is still, to him, the
giant's sword—there is none like that, give it me.

Will you place yourself, you who are an Old Edmundian, in some such position of retrospect, and let your
mind focus itself upon some incident, some impression,
some crisis of your school time ? Not on the common
memories which you will be talking over later in the
day, about the rules which you broke, and the pro-
fessors whose lives you made uncomfortable : dig
deeper, and bring to light some aspect of your boyhood
which you have never discussed, except perhaps in
the confessional. The moment, it may be, or the
period at which you realized and accepted your vocation to the priesthood. Hitherto, you had taken it for
granted you were to be a priest ; then the awkward
age came, and with it difficulties, temptations ; you
had to fight your way through, perhaps with the
advice of others, perhaps with the light God gave in
answer to your prayer. Or, not aspiring to the priesthood, you nevertheless met on this field the first
onslaught of spiritual difficulties ; doubts, temptations,
falls into sin, what you will. Hitherto, Confessions and
Communions had been scarcely more than a matter of
routine ; now you had an enemy to face, perhaps to
dislodge, and you paused a little longer over your
prayers in front of the statue or the shrine. Try to
recapture some such experience, and from it take heart
for whatever needs, whatever dangers you experience
now. The love of Christ and of his Blessed Mother
you learned here ; the sword you killed the giant with.
Say to yourself : There is none like that ; give it me.

Meanwhile, may I address myself to present Edmundians, in so far as I still claim their attention? You have been born into an age of decision for the world and for the Catholic Church. Before our very eyes the half-faiths and the false Christianities which the Reformation brought with it are crumbling away. The number of their adherents is steadily diminishing, and even those who do profess to adhere to them are more and more abandoning belief in the Bible, belief in revelation, belief in the Sacraments, belief in a world of rewards and punishments hereafter. And it is not only their beliefs but their moral standards that are disappearing. Especially the sanctity of marriage is being profaned ; divorce is treated as a natural occurrence ; no age before ours has so openly and so flagrantly set at nought the ordinance of God. And, while Protestantism crumbles away, the Catholic Church is winning back lost ground. We Catholics, in our effort to convert England, are not like furniture removers, paid by the hour, slowly and gingerly piling things on to a van. We are like men fighting a fire, desperately keeping at bay, here and there, the flames of unbelief and of social disorder, while we hurriedly rescue all that we have time to rescue. The fire will get ahead of us if we stop to contemplate our work.

In such an age, to aspire to the priesthood is not to aspire to comforts or to earthly rewards. You do not want to be a priest who simply does his job and knows his rubrics and hopes to pay off a bit of the parish debt. You want to be an ambassador from God to men, ready to take every opening, to follow up every trail, where there is a human conscience to be enlightened or a lost soul to be won back. You want to love souls ; if you do not love souls, you will be hard put to it, in a world of so many temptations, to save your own.

And even if the priesthood has no place in your ambitions, you must still want to leave St. Edmund's not as a Catholic merely, but as a fighting Catholic and a working Catholic. It is possible nowadays, thank God, for laymen to take a direct and public part in spreading the faith. But even apart from that, we Catholics do not live, as our grandfathers used to live, in a sort of water-tight compartment, separated from the world around us. We mix freely with Protestant neighbours, and either we shall influence them or they us. If we are not strongly fortified in the practice of religion, their unbelief will tell upon our faith, their low standard of morality will infect and degrade our consciences. It is becoming a clear issue in our day, the Church or nothing. Do you remember what the priest said to David about the giant's sword ? ' If thou wilt take this, take it ; for there is none other but this.' So it is with the religion you are taught here : there is none other but this. The doctrines which you are taught in apologetics or Christian doctrine class are not a sort of continuation of the gender rhymes ; the practices of piety in which you are encouraged are not a tiresome regulation made for you by house masters. They are the world's last hope, which is committed to your keeping. They are the giant's sword, with which you now face the temptations of boyhood, with which you will face later the temptations of manhood. If thou wilt take this, take it, for there is none other than this.

David was an outlaw in his own country ; you, too, if you are faithful Catholics, still more if you are preaching the Catholic religion, will be outlaws to some extent in the world of to-day, a world which tends more and more to banish religion from its speech and its thought. Other schools have other traditions—

this one has bred great soldiers, this has been a nursery of poets, there the civic virtues are practised and extolled. Our tradition is a different one, and in these days, I think, a more important one. We are a college of outlaws ; those who have gone out from us were men who could set their face against the false standards of the world they lived in, who could stem the current of their times instead of being carried away with it. The names which we record here, with honour and with gratitude, are not those of men whom the world recognized, men who ruled empires or moulded the thought of their day, but those of exiles condemned as traitors, men who loved England too well to leave England what it was. The College has seen many changes, and may see more, but one thing remains constant about our tradition, that the man who is ready to let the world dictate its beliefs to him is a bad Edmundian.

He at least would tell us so, whose festival we keep, whose relics we venerate here. He would tell us that even in a world avowedly Catholic, a world obedient in every outward observance to the discipline of our holy faith, the widest learning, the most cloistered humility, the most single-hearted sincerity of purpose are no protection against hatred, and calumny, and misunderstanding. He has loved justice and hated iniquity, *therefore* he dies in exile—the grim irony of that word 'therefore' should be the Edmundian's armour against the world. He lives and dies an exile who will not take the world at its own valuation, who despises its folly and protests against its wrongs. Even if there were no hereafter to reward us, could we doubt where the man's part lies, which standard beckons us to more adventure, the world's standard or Christ's ? But we must not face that battle in blind confidence ; we must learn to hold and to wield our boyhood's sword, the religion of the Catholic Church. If thou wilt take this, take it, for there is none other than this. And he said : There is none like that ; give it me.

VIII. ST. ALBERT THE GREAT

(Preached at Blackfriars, Oxford.)

Every scribe instructed in the kingdom of heaven is like to a man that is a householder, who bringeth forth out of his treasure new things and old. *Matthew* xiii, 52.

MY text is one of those which we are accustomed to carry in our heads without remembering the occasion upon which the utterance was made, and, partly for that reason, to hesitate about the precise meaning we should attach to it. It comes, actually, at the end of that great chapter, his thirteenth, in which St. Matthew has collected for us seven of our Lord's parables, six of which, if not all seven, deal with the growth of his kingdom, the Church ; the sower, the cockle among the wheat, the mustard seed, the leaven, the hidden treasure, the merchant seeking pearls, the net cast into the sea. And four are particularly concerned to point out to our Lord's hearers that his kingdom was not, as some of them imagined, to be a clean sweep of all that went before it, a complete break-away from all human experience. It was not to be a millennium, in which all sin and suffering would have disappeared ; those who were partakers of it would not be all perfect souls, already confirmed in goodness and destined for eternal life. No, the new kingdom or *ecclesia* of Christ was to be in some ways like the old *ecclesia*, the old congregation of the Jews. There would still be tares among the wheat, worthless fish amongst the catch, side by side with the others. Our Lord, therefore, is not exactly creating a new thing in the world when he lays the foundations of his Church ; in a sense he is only reconstituting, on a new basis and with more extended possibilities, the old *ecclesia* of the Jews which he called to himself so long ago. Do the apostles understand that ? They do ? Good, then they are scribes instructed in the kingdom of heaven ; they see that every new thing in human history is built against the background of some older thing which went before it. As the picture gallery of some great house preserves the memory of its ancestry, tracing down to the latest instance the persistence of the same characteristics, and linking up the present with the past ; so the greatest institutions of the world are those which combine something ancient with something new. And among these, even the Catholic Church.

It is a human weakness of ours to be always crying out for complete novelty, an entire disseverance from our past. Our old traditions have become so dusty with neglect, so rusted with abuse, that we are for casting them on the scrap-heap and forgetting that they ever existed. The Church conserves ; she bears traces still of the Jewish atmosphere in which she was cradled ; traces, too, of the old heathen civilization which she conquered. And in her own history it is the same ; nothing is altogether forgotten ; every age of Christianity recalls the lineaments of an earlier time. People think of her as if she kept a lumber-room ; it is not so ; hers is a treasure-house from which she can bring forth when they are needed things old as well as new.

It is not difficult to see how all this applies to the

history of the thirteenth century, and the reinstatement of Aristotle's philosophy by St. Albert and St. Thomas. The first instinct of Christendom had been to neglect and to disparage the pagan authors, whose works were so saturated with allusions to an idolatrous worship. St. Jerome was afraid of being too good a Ciceronian to be a Christian ; and St. Augustine was ashamed of having been moved to tears by the story of the Aeneid. Buried away in libraries, the works of the ancients slept on ; there is no clear proof that the great library of Alexandria, for instance, suffered much from Christian hands. But the libraries had been collected in the East, and when the East passed under the dominion of Islam, Islam became, for better or worse, the world's librarian. So it was that when Aristotle returned to Europe he returned in Oriental guise, translated and interpreted by the sectaries of the False Prophet. His works were not only dusty with the neglect of centuries, they were corroded with the rust of heretical contamination. Is it wonderful that the Christian world mistrusted their influence ? You have to imagine, if you seek for a modern parallel, a situation in which all the available scientific literature of the world should be in the hands of Soviet Russia, and accessible only in the form of editions scrawled over with Bolshevist comment. It was a heroic adventure, only made possible through the guidance of the Holy Spirit when the theologians of a new order, which still had its reputation for orthodoxy to establish, took upon themselves to make a niche for Aristotle in the ante-chambers of Christian thought. The old weapon, soiled and rusty, useless, you would have thought—but there were men ready to scour and polish it, and make use of it, an instrument as keen as ever, for the confuting of false doctrine and the systematization of knowledge.

New things and old—St. Albert, as a scribe instructed in the Kingdom of Heaven, realized perhaps more than most men of his day that the secular sciences had great advances still to make, and that there must be room for new discoveries in any philosophy which was to express fully the thought of mankind. It was an age unfriendly to research for many reasons. The best brains were either devoted to practical administration in the world, or to theological studies in the cloister ; the tools of science, though they had already been dreamt of, had not yet been forged ; above all, printing had not yet appeared, with all its opportunities for garnering the fruit of human speculation. And the men of to-day will speak in contemptuous terms of the medieval world, as one in which research made no progress ; they forget the difficulties which I have just mentioned ; they forget also that St. Albert was characteristic of his period no less than St. Thomas. And St. Albert certainly had the build of mind which goes to make the research worker. If he had enjoyed more leisure from controversy and from the cares of administration, he would be remembered, as Roger Bacon is remembered, as part of that false dawn of science which went before the Renaissance ; and he would be honoured to-day for activities which he himself would have been the last to think important. But they are important, for this reason if for no other —they prove that the Middle Ages, in taking over Aristotle as their master, did not suppose he had said the last word on every possible subject of discussion. St. Albert was too good an Aristotelian to think that Aristotle must be always right ; he would imitate his master, not merely by borrowing opinions from him, but by instituting original research as he did.

To-day, perhaps more than ever before, the world is eager to make a clean sweep of its past. The war has driven a deep furrow across human experience, separating all that went before it from all that has come and that is to come after it, hardly with less of decisiveness than the Flood in earlier civilizations, than the Christian era in later times. Because we are in a mess with our economics, because Russia has shewn the way to infidelity, because Europe is feeling after a new solidarity, this post-War world feels a different world to us elder people, and our juniors are not slow to rub it in. They talk, they write, as if the world of Einstein and Jeans and Rutherford and Eddington were a world re-born ; as if every earlier guess after the truth were now superseded or exploded ; as if, for the first time, we had begun to know. In such ears, what use to celebrate the praises of St. Albert ? The very name sounds worse than medieval ; it sounds Victorian.

That is the secret of the modern world's antipathy towards the Christian religion, and towards the Catholic Church in particular. They hate it not because it is something arrogant, not because it is something uncomfortable, not because it is something foreign, but because it is something out of date. They know that it will always bring new things and old out of its treasure-house, will not consent to the modern worship of the modern. And they know that there is strength in this deeply rooted tradition which can yet absorb, as it has absorbed all through the ages, lessons that are new. *Stat magni nominis umbra* : they feel, when they meet us, that though they may have heard the last of Albert the Good, they have not heard the last of Albert the Great. A hundred years back they hoped to dispose of the Church by disposing of the Bible ; now their tactics have grown more subtle. They hope to dispose of the Church by disposing of Aristotle. It has become the fashion to gird at us because our whole thought is built up round a philosophical system which was fifteen hundred years old when we assimilated it, and has now ceased to hold the speculative allegiance of mankind. Only the other day I read a book by a popularizer of science, well known in the broadcasting world, whose whole thesis was that Einstein has shewn up Euclid, and if we are not going to believe in Euclid it would be absurd to believe in Aristotle, and if we no longer believe in Aristotle, then Christianity has ceased to count.

It is with happy omen, then, if we may dare to criticize the solemn actions of the Church in terms of human congruity, that the Holy Father has just raised St. Albert to the altars of the Church, and numbered him among her doctors. Not in the sense that the Church is concerned to applaud the physical speculations of the great philosopher, or to regard them as final, when St. Albert himself was not content to regard them as final. Nor even in the sense that Aristotle's metaphysics are the only possible framework of thought in which the Christian world-idea can be stated. Rather because, in the speculative confusion of our time, when men talk as if the theories advanced by natural science were inconsistent with the doctrines of our faith, it is good to look back on a time when Aristotle himself seemed to be an anti-Christian writer, and the attempt to rehabilitate him was regarded with deep suspicion by the old-fashioned. Rather because, when the cry is all for novelty, for further discoveries which shall sweep us away, more and more, from our intellectual bearings, it is well to be reminded that sooner or later human thought always turns back on itself, and the system which was once discredited creeps back into favour again. The modern world lives on its intellectual capital, exploits the prevalent doctrine of the moment in the interest of its heresies ; floodlights the universe with a gleam of partial illumination, or darkens the skies with doubt ; the Church, who is wiser and older, stores new things and old alike in her treasure-house, and brings them out in their due relation to enrich, permanently, the experience of mankind.

May we go further, and admire the Providence which has left it for a Pope, pre-eminently a man of thought as well as a man of action, to canonize a Saint who was pre-eminently a man of action as well as a man of thought ? For, after all, the really surprising thing about St. Albert is not so much the enormous range of learning which won him his title of the Universal Doctor, as the fact that the life which included so much reading and writing, in days when reading and writing were difficult, included also a vast amount of administrative activity ; he was not a mere lecturer or regent of studies ; he was Provincial of his order in Germany, and for three years a bishop. Well might a contemporary describe him as ' the astonishment and miracle of our times.' How did he manage it all ? The secret is out at last ; he was a Saint. The tradition of him preserved in his own order and in his own country has been ratified by the solemn judgement of the Church. Too long we have thought of him as merely reflecting the rays of St. Thomas' beatitude ; we know now that those who were so intimately associated in their lives, and not divided in their loyalty by death, were not divided, save by a few years, in their entry into a blessed eternity. Master and pupil, they could share with our Blessed Lord and our Blessed Lady the joys of an everlasting reunion.

May St. Albert's prayers bring peace to a distracted Europe ; may they enlighten, as he himself enlightened in his time, the darkness of human thought. And

may your own order, Reverend Fathers, be worthy of
its saintly heritage, and prove ever fertile of scribes
instructed in the kingdom of heaven, to bring out of
your treasure-house new things and old.

IX. ROGER BACON

(Preached at his memorial tablet, on the site of the old
Franciscan Friary at Oxford.)

There shall be no remembrance of the wise, no more than of the fool,
for ever ; and the times to come shall cover all things together with
oblivion. The learned dieth in like manner as the unlearned.
Ecclesiastes ii, 16.

ROGER BACON, whose memory is perpetuated
by that tablet in the wall in front of you, is one
of the world's great men. He left behind him a
living tradition, in Oxford especially ; so that men
looked back to him as if he had been a great magician,
something like Doctor Faustus ; and you may still
see prints of the gate-house that used to stand on
Folly Bridge, which is described, in the legend underneath the picture, as Friar Bacon's study. But while
his memory in men's mouths thus passed into something legendary, his works remained scattered through
the libraries of Europe ; probably there are more
of them to be unearthed yet. And as these were found
and published he acquired a new reputation in the
learned world, as if he had been a man vastly ahead
of his time, both in the methods of his research and
the results of it. Not because of his most characteristic

views, the views he expressed with most warmth
and courage ; as, for example, that the philosophers
of his day were all taking the wrong course because
they could not study the works of older philosophers
in the original Greek and Arabic ; or that theology
was at fault because it was not strictly based on a
careful examination of Holy Scripture, which was,
to Roger Bacon, the ultimate source of all knowledge
whatsoever. No, the moderns have been interested
in Bacon because he did know something about
optics, could tell you how to make a telescope or
a microscope, though it does not appear that he
had either ; dreamed, perhaps, of steam traction
a.ad of aviation, had a secret recipe for making gun-
powder ; sought, even, in the very latest fashion, to
set out all physical reality in mathematical formulæ.
One of the world's great men ; we do well to put
up a tablet to him.

At the same time, Roger Bacon is not a Saint.
He is not, that is to say, a Saint canonized by the
Church ; we can never say with certainty that this
man or that, who has died, is not reigning already
in heaven ; only God knows that, who can read our
consciences. But the character of Bacon, as you
find it in his own writings or in the impressions of
his contemporaries, is not apt to strike the reader
as a saintly character. Indeed, if the truth must be
told, within earshot, almost, of all these venerable
institutions, Bacon was not much of a Saint—he
was more of a don. He had the don's unalterable
conviction that all the other dons were going the
wrong way about things ; that they were not profound enough, not accurate enough ; that nothing
could be done until the whole of learning had been
reorganized on his own lines. It was not that Bacon
was attempting to glorify his own order by belittling

the work of other orders ; he was quite as fierce about
Alexander of Hales, the Franciscan, as about anybody
else. And if he lived a troubled life, and incurred
the suspicion of his superiors, it is difficult not to
believe that it was partly his own fault. He had the
irritable temperament of the scholar, and he minced
no words when he wanted to put other people
right.

But although he may not have been a Saint, Bacon
was a perfectly good Catholic. He was, in every
way, a child of his age. It is very tempting, but it
is a great mistake to hail him as the prophet born
out of due time, who anticipated this or that later
movement, and deserves to be regarded as the father
of it. He wanted to revive the study of Greek, but
he is not the fore-runner of humanism ; he cared
nothing for the classical culture, he only wanted
people to read Aristotle, and the New Testament,
in the original. He believed in getting back to Scripture, but he was not the forerunner of the Reformation. On the contrary, he was befriended by a Pope,
and everywhere treats the papacy with due respect ;
nor is his complaint against the worldliness of Bishops
or prelates, but against the ignorance of scholars.
He shews a wonderful *flair* for science when you
consider the limited possibilities that existed in his
day for the study of it ; but he is not the forerunner
of the Empiricists ; has no kinship with his namesake,
Francis. To him, as to all the men of his day, metaphysics was the highest form of science in the human
scale ; and metaphysics was only the handmaid
of theology. If Roger Bacon came back to Oxford
to-day I believe you would find him quarrelling
with all the other learned men as heartily as ever.
The philosophers would find him a back number
and the scholars would find him a pedant, and the

scientists would find him a chopper of logic, and the theologians would find him a fundamentalist; and there would be fresh trouble all round.

But Roger Bacon is dead. And by that I do not mean merely that his soul long since underwent separation from his body, as all souls must. I mean that his very memory is by now a thing of the past, belongs to an old world, which is still the subject of antiquarian interest, but is not near enough to us to feel as if it were a part of ourselves. With the Saints, you see, it is otherwise; just as their bodies, in many cases, have been found uncorrupt long years after they were buried, so their lives remain embalmed for us in the odour of sanctity, belong to us, if we are faithful Catholics, as if they were men of yesterday. Saint Francis is not dead, in the sense in which I am now using the word. He is removed from our company, because he is in heaven; but his story is of yesterday; he is like an elder brother who died, more is the pity, before we were born. You cannot think of him as remote, uncongenial, shut off from us; his sanctity bridges the centuries that lie between us. But Roger Bacon belongs to the past, for all those precocious speculations of his which made him seem ahead of his time. There shall be no remembrance of the wise, no more than of the fool, for ever; and the times to come shall cover all things together with oblivion. The learned dieth in like manner as the unlearned. That is the law under which Roger Bacon is forgotten.

And yet, is he forgotten? Not altogether; not in Oxford. He is remembered here because his own Grey Friars have come back here and will not allow the site of their old residence to be altogether obliterated. So they have chosen Brother Roger

as the type, the representative, of all those many
Franciscan friars who must be waiting, not far from
this spot, for their Resurrection. We are to pray,
not 'grant him,' but 'grant them' eternal rest ;
not only Brother Roger, but all those cloister-mates
of his whose names we do not know ; the ones who
worked for him without acknowledgment, copied
out manuscripts for him and verified facts for him
and pointed out slips he had made, helped in one
way and another to make his name the great name
it is ; the ones who did not quite approve of him,
and thought his studies were all waste of time, if
not worse ; the ones who laughed at him, and thought
him a crack-brained old fellow ; the learned people
(for there were plenty of others in that beautiful
dawn of Oxford scholarship) who never managed
to achieve fame like his, and the simple people who
were content to be simple people like St. Francis
—all the old Grey Friars you must have seen once,
walking up and down behind the old battlements,
as you came upon Oxford from the south, across
the windings of the Thames.

All alike, Brother Roger with the rest of them,
belong to the past now ; the conditions under which
they lived, the problems they had to face, were not
our conditions or our problems, and we cannot
really put ourselves in their place, or them in ours.
The world is so full of anxiety about the present,
of speculation about the future, that it has no time
to waste, no tears to shed, over the ruined glories
of the past. But we, Catholics of Oxford, assemble
once a year to remember these fellow-townsmen,
fellow-gownsmen of ours, and to pray for their souls ;
that gracious bond of unity is not destroyed for us
by any lapse of years or any change of manners.
Let us commend, then, to the mercy of God and

to the prayers of his Blessed Mother that restless
soul, so long ago laid to rest, and the souls of all who
in times past ministered or worshipped in this place ;
and let us pray also, in this place, for a restoration
to the university of the faith in which it was cradled,
and of the sacramental life which it once lived by,
and has lost.

X. ST. JOAN OF ARC

(Preached to schoolboys at St. Edmund's, Ware.)

All these died according to faith, not having received the promises,
but beholding them afar off and saluting them, and confessing that
they are pilgrims and strangers on the earth. . . . Who by faith conquered kingdoms, wrought justice, obtained promises, stopped the
mouths of lions, quenched the violence of fire, escaped the edge of the
sword, recovered strength from weakness, became valiant in battle,
put to flight the armies of foreigners. *Hebrews* xi, 13, 33, 34.

I DO not know how it is with you, but, for me,
almost ever since I can remember hearing it read,
this chapter of the Hebrews has exercised a special
fascination, has enabled me to follow the story of
the Old Testament in a new attitude and with a
new interest. The patriarchs as you knew them
when you were quite small, whether from picture-
books or from the confirmatory evidence supplied
by stained-glass windows, were old gentlemen with
beards who had their clothes, mostly in rather dowdy
purples and browns, hitched up round them in an
inconvenient sort of way, and always carried a large
stick in one hand and a thurible in the other when,
apparently, they were just going out for a walk.
Heavy, lifeless figures they seemed, against a flat,

conventional background of palm-trees, and you felt it was impossible that they should ever mean anything to you or carry any living message. And then came this chapter of the Hebrews and filled the whole scene with life, set the cardboard palm-trees waving and the long skirts rustling, and everything was astir. It was not simply that they went to the same tailor, they had something in common ; there was a secret behind their dignified silence. They died according to faith, not having received the promises, but beholding them afar off and saluting them ; God providing some better thing for us, that without us they should not be perfected.

By faith he—that is, Abraham—abode in the land, dwelling in tents with Isaac and Jacob, the co-heirs of the same promise ; for he looked for a city that hath foundations, whose builder and maker is God. He managed to live in tents, to endure that uncomfortable, makeshift, draughty sort of existence—how ? Because he looked for a city that hath foundations, whose builder and maker is God. That is the faith of the Old Testament Saints, to live as strangers in a transitory world on the strength of a promise—a promise they knew they would not live to see fulfilled. Faith is the substance of things hoped for, the evidence of things that appear not. And you will find that same common quality among the Saints of the Christian dispensation. They lived in very different ages and very different countries ; their circumstances differed widely, and their manner of life. Yesterday we had the office of St. John Baptist de la Salle, who rose to sanctity in the exercise of a very humble and a very humdrum occupation, and one that does not often produce Saints : he was a schoolmaster. And to-day the infallible Voice of Christendom is raising to the altars of the Church, as she was long since raised to the glories of heaven, the heroine of a very different career : a village girl who really did conquer kingdoms, really did recover strength from weakness, became valiant in battle, put to flight the armies of foreigners—yes, St. Joan of Arc. How nice it sounds, ' St. Joan of Arc.' But through all the history of sanctity you will find this same quality persisting—the quality of realizing that what we see and touch and feel are transitory things and unreal, and that the solid things, the substantial things, are the things that appear not, the world we only grasp by faith.

And I am insisting on that particular quality this morning because I think it is one that stands out with quite extraordinary clearness in St. Joan's life : she did really live for a promise, and we know that the promise came true, but she did not—not in this life. She was very young, you know. Did you realize that she was less than twenty years old when she was burnt at the stake ? It is not true that she dressed as a man ; she dressed as a boy. When she was only thirteen years old, at the age when the other boys and girls were fidgeting and playing the fool during Mass, as people did in those days, she could hardly go out of doors without hearing the voices of Saints and Angels talking to her. And those voices dominated her life ; they echoed so loudly in her ears that all the world's noises were drowned for her. People said : ' It is very silly of a small girl like you to think she can go and see the King '—she did not hear them. And the King, as you know, disguised himself and hid among his courtiers, and she went straight up to him : ' But I am not the King,' he said, ' that is the King over there.' ' Oh, yes, you are ; I have come to raise the siege of Orleans and crown you king at Rheims.'

It was no good ; the voices had told her about it.
And I suppose when she had been appointed Chief
of the Army the General Staff would always be raising
military difficulties about re-entrant angles and being
enfiladed by arquebus-fire, and so on, but it did not
make a bit of difference to her, she always did what
the voices told her—they were close to her ear, you
see, and the criticisms of the General Staff were
only a distant echo. She went out, not knowing
whither she went.

And of course she had disappointments. After
the first few victories, after the crowning of the King,
the people she had come to save contented themselves
with a partial conquest, and hung about making
treaties and demobilizing troops. And truly, if she
had been mindful of that from whence she came
out, she had doubtless time to return ; she could
have gone back to Domrémy and rested on her
laurels. But the ingratitude and apathy of the court
affected her no more than its honours had done ;
she simply went on obeying the voices. And the
French lords played her false, and she was taken
prisoner. But she endured, as seeing him who is
invisible.

And then came the hardest time of all. I do not
think she minded being in prison ; I do not think
she minded the threat of execution ; that was not
why she tried to escape. No, it was simply that it
seemed quite obvious to her she was to deliver France
—the voices had told her so—and France was not
yet delivered. And so she went to the stake, her
hopes still unfulfilled, but never doubting for an
instant that the voices were true. Five years later
the King entered Paris ; twenty-two years later,
England had no possessions left on French soil. She
believed that he was faithful who had promised,

not having received the promises, but beholding them afar off and saluting them. She could not foresee that her unjust condemnation would be reversed, point by point, twenty-five years after her death : she could not foresee that, nearly five hundred years after her death, France, once more liberated, would receive the tidings of her canonization by the tribunal to which, in life, she never ceased to appeal, the tribunal of the Holy See. But she believed that he was faithful who had promised.

That, then, is her great witness, as it is the witness of all the Saints : that is her capital contribution to our Christian hope—we know, because the Saints have told us so, that it is the things of this world that are shams and shadows, and the real things and the solid things are the things we cannot see. Our Saviour Christ has ascended up into heaven, and a cloud received him from our sight, but we are not therefore to think of the spiritual world as something far removed from us, only to be reached by a supreme effort of thought. On the contrary, the spiritual world is all about us : the voices are still there, only St. Joan could hear them and we cannot. I wonder whose fault that is ? Blessed are the pure in heart, for they shall see God.

> The Angels keep their ancient places ;
>   Turn but a stone, and start a wing :
> 'Tis ye, 'tis your estranged faces
>   That miss the many-splendoured thing.
> But, when so sad thou canst not sadder,
>   Cry, and upon thy so sore loss
> Shall shine the traffic of Jacob's ladder
>   Pitched between Heaven and Charing Cross.

This is no other but the house of God, and the gate of Heaven. When we keep, as to-day, the festival of the Dedication of a Church, this earthly edifice is a sort of sacrament to us, a type of the true city which hath foundations, whose builder and maker is God : of the temple that is built in a world beyond the reach of our sense, by a heavenly Architect, the blows of whose mallet, the polishing strokes of whose chisel, we call pain in this world, and defeat, and loss. Whither may God of his great mercy bring us, that we may see with open vision, among the choir of Virgins that are our Lady's handmaids, the Saint whose glorious merits the Church commemorates to-day.

XI. KING HENRY THE SIXTH

(Preached at St. Catharine's, Chipping Campden.)

These are they whom we had some time in derision, and for a parable of reproach. We fools esteemed their life madness, and their end without honour. Behold, how they are numbered among the children of God, and their lot is among the saints. *Wisdom* v, 3.

FOUR hundred and fifty-five years since, a week ago last Saturday, died the only king of England since the Conquest who has ever been within measurable distance of being raised to the altars of the Church. And because, in our day, there is some hope that his cause will be proceeded with afresh after a long lapse of centuries ; because I am particularly bound to him as the Founder of the school at which I was educated, I want to represent to you very briefly this morning the true facts about King Henry the Sixth, and to ask —if what you hear interests you—your prayers for his eventual beatification.

King Henry the Sixth ? The mind fumbles ner-

vously in the dusty pigeon-holes of memory. Echoes
from the small green Gardiner respond unwillingly to
the call. Yes, Henry the Sixth, let me see, was not he
the king who was always going mad ? An innocent
creature, to be sure, not responsible for all the
calamities which befell England during his reign ; his
murder in prison was, I quite agree, one of the most
brutal in English history. But . . . a Saint ? Surely
this harmless type of character, under-developed and
barely capable for better or worse of moral action, has
nothing to do with the manly virtues of the Saints ?
They felt temptation, and triumphed over it ; they
dominated their fellow-men, left their mark on the
world through sheer force of character. Surely you are
not going to set up this weakling, this half-idiot,
beside men like Dunstan, and Anselm, and Thomas
More ?

These are they whom we had in derision, and for a
parable of reproach. We fools esteemed their life
madness, and their end without honour. Behold, how
they are numbered among the children of God, and
their lot is among the Saints. . . . Let me tell you a
story. Possibly it is not true, but it is a story which
was affirmed on oath and duly chronicled at the time.
A little while after King Henry the Sixth died, when it
had begun to be rumoured that miracles were being
wrought through his prayers, a near neighbour of
yours, a certain John Robins of Inkberrow, was
making his way to Stratford-on-Avon. And it will
have been soon after Abbot's Moreton, where he
turned into the main road, that he met with another
countryman, George Luffar from Crowle, who began
to talk to him about the holy King Henry and his
wonderful miracles. I daresay George Luffar was a
tiresome enthusiast, but anyhow John Robins got
weary of it, said he did not believe a word of it, said

that King Henry was just an innocent creature who hardly knew his right hand from his left, and no more a Saint than anyone else. And so they went on arguing until they got to Stratford. The same day, while he was in Stratford, John Robins went stone blind. There was no explanation of it, and there was no cure for it, until he vowed that he would make a pilgrimage to King Henry's tomb at Windsor—a vow which was afterwards duly paid—and then he recovered his sight on the spot.

Well, I would not trouble you with that story if it were the only story of its kind. But it is one out of one hundred and seventy-four similar stories which are preserved for us in a manuscript now kept at the British Museum. And we know, from that manuscript, that in St. George's Chapel at Windsor they kept a list which contained the record of at least three hundred and sixty-eight miraculous cures and deliverances as the result of prayers offered to King Henry; all of which date during the thirty years between his death in 1471 and the end of that century. What does it all mean? It means that at the end of the fifteenth century the pilgrimage to Windsor was one of the great English pilgrimages, like those to St. Thomas at Canterbury and our Lady at Walsingham. It means that in churches all over the country pictures and statues of King Henry were being put up as if he were one of the Saints—a dozen or so of them may still be seen to-day—that lights were kept burning, and hymns were written in his honour. It means that in those days the natural thing to do, if you were in any trouble, was to appeal to a dead king for his prayers. Why, in the reign of Richard the Third, who was King Henry's murderer, there was a girl over at Honeybourne, called Agnes Freeman, who suffered from what was called the King's Evil; it was a skin disease which could be cured, men said, only by the touch of the reigning monarch—and so it continued down to the day when Dr. Johnson was touched for the King's Evil by Queen Anne. But Agnes Freeman did not go to Richard the Third ; she went to the dead king's tomb instead, and found relief from her malady there.

Now, it is quite true that King Henry is not the only popular hero who has been regarded as a Saint by the people who could remember him. The body of Simon de Montfort, the leader of the Barons against the king two hundred years earlier, was kept in the Abbey Church at Evesham, and there is record of miracles happening there. But there is this difference, you see ; the devotion to Simon de Montfort died out : the devotion to King Henry did not die out, it was simply swamped by the Reformation. In 1528, the year before Thomas Cranmer became Archbishop of Canterbury, it is historically certain that the envoys of King Henry the Eighth at Rome, while they were urging the Pope to sanction the divorce from Catherine of Aragon, were also urging him to proceed with the beatification of King Henry the Sixth. And the Pope was perfectly willing, he was only waiting for the arrival of fresh evidence from England. And that evidence never came, because the breach between England and Rome came first. The cause had dropped, but the devotion to King Henry did not drop. It is historically certain that pilgrims from Devonshire and Cornwall were coming in large numbers all the way to Windsor as late as the year 1543. 1543, that is nearly seventy years after King Henry the Sixth died, and only half a dozen years before the Mass was abolished in England. England did not lose her faith in King Henry until she lost her faith in the Catholic Church.

Well, I have taken the risk of giving you all this dull lecture in history because, as I say, the reopening of the cause at Rome after nearly four hundred years does seem to be practical politics just now. But nothing will come of it unless people in England will offer prayers for that intention. After all, St. Joan of Arc was neglected for more than four hundred years and then canonized ; and now that England, more than ever since the Reformation, is beginning to count among the Catholic countries of Europe, it would be a pity if through some want of patriotism, some want of feeling for our Catholic past, we missed the opportunity of publicly invoking a Saint of our own royal lineage. Pray, then, for his beatification, you who love the English countryside which he loved ; and commit to him sometimes your prayers for temporal or spiritual favours ; if experience goes for anything, it will not be in vain.

We esteemed their life madness. It is true that twice, during the fifty years of his life, King Henry was deprived, for a time, of the use not only of his senses, but apparently of his limbs. The attack, upon either occasion, lasted less than two months. For the rest, although he was a weak king in stormy times, nobody ever doubted that he had the full use of his reason. The founder of Eton, and of King's College, Cambridge—and in either case he drew up the statutes himself, with particular care—has left to the nation a legacy which is more enduring than those of most English monarchs. There was, in his whole character, a child-like innocence which the men of his own day took for sanctity ; it was left for later generations to suggest that this innocence was a form of feeble-mindedness. Is it, perhaps, that in our day we have lost the faculty for appreciating sheer innocence, for understanding the temperament of one who is brutally treated by his enemies, yet bears it all without complaint ? If so, I think that King Henry has yet a work to do in schooling and in softening our English hearts.

XII. ST. THOMAS MORE

Thus did this man die, leaving not only to young men, but also to the whole nation, the memory of his death for an example of virtue and fortitude. 2 *Machabees* vi, 31.

THE text which I have just read to you refers to Eleazar, one of the scribes, who suffered martyrdom under King Antiochus for the traditions of the Jewish religion. As a sign of apostasy from that religion, he, like many others, was bidden to eat swine's flesh, which (as you know) was forbidden under the ancient law. Kindly officials offered him, instead, a piece of some other meat which was clean according to the law of Moses ; so that he could avoid the defilement as long as he would allow it to be thought that he had conformed with Antiochus' edict. His answer was a noble one ; he would rather suffer martyrdom than give scandal to the younger men of his race by pretending to break the law in his old age. He died, it seems, under scourging.

You will not be at a loss to understand why I am recalling to you, this evening, the memory of unhappy things that took place long ago. The history conveys a striking parallel to other unhappy things which happened not so very long ago, only four hundred years ago yesterday. On July 6, 1535, a great Englishman died who has just been raised to the altars of the

Church as St. Thomas More. He died, like Eleazar, for something which seemed to many people of his time almost a scruple, almost a technical point ; refusing to take an oath in support of a new statute, because there was something in the preamble to the statute of which your conscience disapproved ! Oh, you may be sure that St. Thomas More had no lack of plausible excuses if he had wanted to avoid the crown of martyrdom ; no lack of sincere people who urged him to take refuge in them. Never, I suppose, was man so tempted both by friends and foes to abandon his purpose. His own wife, his own daughter took the part of his enemies, and entered into a loving conspiracy to save him from himself. But to friend and foe alike he opposed the impenetrable wall of his good-natured banter.

You see, he realized, long before other men of his time, that what stood before England was a complete parting of the ways. He saw that, in the conditions of his time, you must needs throw in your lot either with the old faith or with the heresies that were beginning to spring up all over Europe ; that a nation which defied the authority of the Pope, although it might do so merely in the name of national independence, would be forced, sooner or later, into the camp of the heretic. It is amazing to us, looking back upon all the inter- vening centuries have brought, that so many good men of that age—men who were afterwards confessors for the faith—were hoodwinked for the moment into following the King when he incurred the guilt of schism. But perhaps if we could think ourselves back rather more successfully into the conditions of the time, we should pardon them the more readily ; and for that reason we should feel even greater admiration for the few men who, like our martyr, were wise enough to see what was happening. It was a time of national crisis, a time of intellectual ferment. There were only a few people who kept their heads, and those few who kept their heads lost their heads, like St. Thomas More.

Much, naturally, has been said, much has been written in the past few months about him and about the holy Bishop of Rochester who preceded him to his death. His portrait has become familiar to us afresh ; his praises are sounded everywhere, even in the most unlikely quarters. What I should like to draw your attention to, this evening, is a single fact about the life and fame of a many-sided man. This fact—that his canonization has been a bewilderment and a blow to the moderns, precisely because he was himself one of the moderns. He belongs to the new world which came to its birth at the Renaissance ; of that new world he is a prophet and a pioneer. And, being all that, he gave his life, unquestioningly and unquestionably, for something which our moderns look upon as belonging wholly to that older world which is dead— I mean, the Holy Catholic Church.

It is a curious thing about the attitude of our non-Catholic friends towards the Catholic Saints ; they always contrive to discredit, in one of two ways, their witness to the faith. Either they will say : ' This was a very unpleasant, narrow-minded man, of ridiculous personal habits ; and if that is what Saints are like we would sooner hear no more of them,' or they will say : ' Yes, this man was indeed a Saint ; but then he was not really a Roman Catholic. He was just a good Christian, as I and my wife are ; he only happened to be in communion with the Pope because everybody was in those days.' They divide our calendar, in fact, into the nice Saints who do credit to Christianity rather than to the Church, and the nasty Saints who do no credit to anybody. St. Francis, they will say ; yes, what a charming character; what meekness, what cheerfulness, what love of animals! But then, St. Francis was not a bit like a Roman Catholic. On the other hand, a man like St. Thomas à Becket, although they admit that his martyrdom was an unfortunate incident, they dismiss altogether from consideration because his particular qualities, his salient qualities anyhow, were not the particular qualities which they happen to admire. And the Church gets no credit either way.

It is being a great puzzle to these people what to make of St. Thomas More. So long as he was simply Thomas More it was all right; they were prepared to admire him as a pioneer of modern thought, or to praise him as a man who gave his life for his convictions, however mistaken. But now, we have taken to calling him a Saint, and it is difficult to see which of the two categories he is to fit into. Is he to be regarded as one of the Saints who were not really nice men, were not really admirable men? But nobody can help loving Thomas More; nobody can help admiring Thomas More. Or are they going to regard him as one of the Saints who were not really Roman Catholics? But unfortunately, his death makes that impossible. In life, if you will, he can be regarded as one of the moderns, as a pioneer of the Renaissance, as a cultured, liberal, broad-minded man, all that they are prepared to admire. But in his death, look at it what way you will, he is plainly a Catholic. He exploded the mine of controversy twenty-five years before its time; forced an issue between England and the Holy See before England had ever realized that it was going Protestant. Is it possible that we are to have, after all, an indisputably Catholic Saint whom, nevertheless, our non-Catholic neighbours will find themselves compelled to admire?

Let us pause for a little over that apparent contrast in the life of a man whose sympathies clearly belonged to the new order of things, who yet died as a protest on behalf of the old order of things. Let me explain to you, at the risk of seeming to give you a lecture in history, what I mean when I say that St. Thomas More has to take rank among the moderns. Of course, there is a certain sense in which all the English martyrs belong to our modern world, as compared with the English Saints who went before them. If you think of St. Edmund of Canterbury, or St. Richard of Chichester, the last English Saints who lived before Reformation times, you inevitably think of them, if I may say so without irreverence, as people in stained-glass windows, belonging to an era altogether different from our own. We do not know what they looked like, because there was little art of portraiture in their day, and of the art there was few specimens are preserved to us. And the medieval world to which they belonged is something we read about in history books, but something which has, so it appears, no living contact with our own. But our martyrs, even under Henry the Eighth and Queen Elizabeth, are living, human figures ; in many cases we have authentic portraits, their writings have come down to us in abundance— we can imagine, or so we think, what it was like to live under the Tudors. Yes, the English martyrs are nearer to us than the Saints who went before them ; but in the case of St. Thomas More it goes deeper than that. He was a humanist, one of the most prominent figures in that revival of learning, that broadening of culture, which followed upon what we call the Renaissance. All that, you say, is very vague ; I am using long words, which leave no particular impression on your mind. Very well, then, let me try to put it in the concrete a little, and consider how it was that the men

of the Renaissance differed from the men of the
Middle Ages.

First, the men of the Renaissance looked backwards
at history more than their predecessors did. The old
classical authors of Greece and Rome, long hidden
away in the shelves of dusty libraries, came to light and
were studied eagerly. They tried to feel and to understand what other men thought, long centuries ago
before our Lord came. And St. Thomas More was
steeped in all that ; although he was such a busy man
of affairs, he was one of the scholars of his age, the
intimate friend of the great Dutchman, Erasmus.
Many historians will tell you that the Renaissance, by
opening men's minds to new avenues of learning,
paved the way for the Reformation. It may be so,
but among the greatest leaders of the Renaissance you
will find St. Thomas More, who died a martyr for the
Catholic faith.

In the second place, the men of the Renaissance
looked outwards at a world that had grown larger
than the world which their fathers knew. ' The world,'
as it was known to the Middle Ages, meant—what ?
Europe, and the north coast of Africa, and a few
strange, half-fabulous countries in the East, which
only a few unreliable travellers had visited. By the
year 1500 Columbus had discovered America, Cabot
had sailed to Canada, and Vasco da Gama had
doubled the Cape of Good Hope. Within a quarter
of a century the known world had suddenly grown to
three or four times its old size. Men's minds were
fascinated by the thought that there were strange
races in distant parts of the earth whose customs and
traditions and way of looking at life were wholly
different from their own. And not least, the mind of
St. Thomas More. Every schoolboy knows that he
wrote a book called *Utopia*, describing the habits of

an imaginary people on some remote island, and using that means to satirize the shortcomings of his own day. That imaginary island owed its existence, you may say, to the discoveries of explorers among real islands, twenty or thirty years before the book was written. The mind of such a man, clearly, was not bounded as men's minds were bounded in the Middle Ages by the horizon of Christendom. And yet it was for Christendom that St. Thomas More died on the scaffold.

In the third place—this is more difficult to explain—the men of the Renaissance looked inwards, turned back upon themselves, watched their own thoughts, instead of being entirely wrapped up in objects outside themselves which challenged their attention. The proper study of mankind, said a great poet, is Man ; and the men of the Renaissance are called Humanists because they rediscovered, in a way, the greatness and the complexity and the absorbing interest of Man. You will find that all through the sixteenth century ; you will find it in the art of Shakespeare, you will find it among the theologians of that age, in the enormously increased study of moral theology. And you will find it in the character of a man like St. Thomas More ; exemplified especially in that gift of self-criticism and of irony which distinguishes him ; what we call nowadays, roughly, the sense of humour. A man passionately interested in men, allowing for their temperaments and sympathizing with their weaknesses. Yet a Humanist, we see, could also be a man of stern principle ; it was because he would not condone the weaknesses of the king who had been his friend that St. Thomas More died.

All that enlargement of outlook, backwards, outwards, inwards, makes St. Thomas More one of the moderns. If he lived in our own day—let us put it

crudely—you can imagine him arguing over Plato
with Dean Inge, or constructing imaginary worlds in
collaboration with Mr. H. G. Wells, or answering jest
with jest, irony with irony, in a conversation with Mr.
Bernard Shaw. And if he had died in his bed, before
the attack on the monasteries, before the question of
King Henry's divorce ever arose, just imagine what the
world would be saying of him. They would be telling
us that he was, of course, a Roman Catholic, because
that was how he had been brought up—indeed, in his
youth he had been through a period of fanaticism, in
which he thought of joining the Carthusians. But his
whole mind, they would be telling us, had completely
outgrown the narrow horizons of his youth ; he was a
critic of abuses in the Church, he was a friend of those
Continental scholars who made, in great part, the
Reformation. And had he lived, they would be
telling us, this patron of the new learning would
certainly have thrown in his lot with the Reformers,
with Cranmer and Cromwell ; perhaps, as an old
man, he would have helped to build up the sonorous
language of the Anglican prayer-book. All that they
would be saying, were it not for the unfortunate fact
that he died a Roman Catholic, died because he was a
Roman Catholic, died because he saw that you could
not be a Catholic without being a Roman.

That seems to me the really extraordinary quality
about our new Saint, that he could bring forth out
of his treasure, like the householder of Our Lord's
parable, things new and old ; that he belonged to
the new world, and yet died for something against
which the new world was shortly to revolt. If he
had been some member of the old English aristocracy,
suspicious of the Tudors because they were upstarts,
and resentful against their efforts to consolidate
the power of the Crown as against the nobility—

then we might have been afraid that political considerations affected his attitude. But it was not so ; he was one of the new men, one of the King's friends, the last man in the world to stand upon ancient privilege for its own sake. If he had been some pedantic follower of a philosophy which had gone out of fashion, resolutely set against all new-fangled ideas, then we might have been afraid that there was something of mere human obstinacy, mere pig-headedness, that entered into his protest. But it was not so ; as we have seen, he was a pillar and a patron of the new learning. If he had been some bluff, rude country squire, always ready to pick a quarrel with his neighbours for the sheer love of a fight, careless of what suffering he underwent himself or inflicted on others, then we might have been afraid that he took the risks he took, faced the scaffold as he did, out of a kind of insensibility, valuing his life little because he had never acquired the art of enjoying life intelligently. But no, St. Thomas More was a sensitive man, of our modern type, very reluctant, as we know, to inflict punishment on others, and fully alive to the horrors of his own situation, as you or I would be. It was not temperament, it was not perversity, but sheer love of the faith he had been bred in that made a martyr of St. Thomas More.

I wonder whether there is not something Providential, I mean something that we can recognize as specially Providential, about the delays which have attended the canonization of St. Thomas More and St. John Fisher, humanly speaking so long overdue ? Whether, I mean, God does not mean us to understand that these two, and St. Thomas More especially, are fitting patrons for our own age, because our own age is in so many ways like theirs ? For in our age—it is a commonplace to say it—a new humanism flourishes, something like the humanism of four hundred years ago, but for better or worse a great advance upon it. We have dug further back than ever St. Thomas More and his contemporaries did into the history of our race ; unearthed the relics of civilizations far older than those of Greece or Rome, pushed back, by tens of thousands of years, the limits of human history. We have not discovered fresh continents—there were none to discover ; but we have entered into closer contact with men of alien ideas, studied their history, and puzzled out the secret of their attitude towards life. And we have turned back more than ever on ourselves ; analysed the background of our own minds, tried to trace the origins of our own mental processes. Our age, more than ever, is lost in admiration of man's greatness, so as to forget the God who made us ; at the same time, more tender towards man's weaknesses, more tolerant of his wrong-doing, more merciful to his faults. And in this age of increased reverence for man you and I have got to live, reminding ourselves and reminding our neighbours of that higher reverence which is due to God.

Times like these, do not let us deceive ourselves about it, are difficult to live in for a Catholic who loves his faith. There is a continual apparent contrast between the restless speculations of the modern intellect, and those abiding certainties by which we live. The question continually arises : Is such and such a view, which I see propounded in the newspapers, consistent with Catholic truth ? Is such and such a political expedient, which I see prominent men are advocating, justifiable in the light of Catholic doctrine ? We are hurried along breathlessly by the spirit of the age in which we live, yet protesting all the time, questioning all the time. Our neighbours, our non-Catholic neighbours, look upon us as an obscure survival from the Middle Ages, a kind of museum piece, whose beliefs they find it interesting to study, but impossible to share. Here and there, one or two of our Catholic friends drop out of the ranks, abandon their religion for no better reason than that they have been caught by the glamour of modern movements. There is no acute conflict, but we are perpetually ill at ease, like a ship that drags its anchor.

In such times, let us thank God's mercy for giving us the example and the protection of a great Saint, our own fellow-countryman, who knew how to absorb all that was best in the restless culture of his day, yet knew at once, when the time came, that he must make a stand here ; that he must give no quarter to the modern world here. His remembrance has long been secure in the praise of posterity ; it only remained for us to be assured by the infallible voice of the Church, what we could not doubt already, that he is with our Blessed Lady and the Saints in heaven. He knows our modern needs, let us turn to him in our modern troubles ; his prayers will not be lacking for the great country he loved so, for the great city in which he lived and died.

XIII. ST. IGNATIUS LOYOLA

(Preached at Farm Street.)

Then his son Judas, called Machabeus, rose up in his stead ; and all his brethren helped him, and all they that had joined themselves to his father, and they fought with cheerfulness the battle of Israel. 1 *Machabees* iii, 1.

THERE are few stories, I suppose, in history, so epical as that of the resistance made by Juda under the Machabees to the power of Syrian tyrants ; there have been few movements which combined, so perfectly as theirs did, the twin aspirations of religion and patriotism. That the Church holds them in special honour is witnessed by the curious fact that they, almost alone among all the heroes of the Old Testament, have a feast and a Mass and an Office dedicated yearly to their honour. We Catholics are not always very well read in the Old Testament ; let me just remind you briefly, then, of what it was these men did, and what was the quarrel in which they fought.

The conquests of Alexander the Great at the end of the third century before Christ had let loose all over the East, as far as the borders of India, a flood of Greek influence and rather superficial Greek civilization. At his death, his chief captains, like the marshals of Napoleon, ascended royal thrones ; in Egypt, the Ptolemies, in Syria, the Seleuci. When war arose between these two dynasties, as it did a generation later, it was inevitable that the little people of Juda, with their territory lying on the high road from Syria to Egypt, should be swept into the current of world politics once more. And that meant grave peril to their national faith, and to their mission as the one people in the world which maintained, in its integrity, the worship of the one true God. Gentile influences began to creep in— the Greek tolerance of false worship and of superstition, the Greek cult of beauty, the Greek contempt for morals. There was a party in Judaea itself favourable to this foreign culture. And when Antiochus Epiphanes came up with an army to Jerusalem, and sacked it, and robbed the temple treasures, and set up heathen worship in the Holy Places, it was not the whole nation that protested and suffered. Some Jews, in that degenerate age, were ready to conform to the new order of things ; they consented to eat the flesh of swine, forbidden to them by the Mosaic law, in witness of their apostasy. But there was a remnant which remained faithful ; and it was these who, under the leadership of the Machabean brethren, won back the holy city, and defeated army after army sent against them by their oppressors, and re-established the independence of their country until it was finally lost through the conquests of the Romans a century later.

I would like you to notice three points especially about the triumphant career of these patriots. The first is this—that we are dealing with a succession of men, all of the same family, who all shewed the same spirit and maintained the same policy with equal fearlessness. You do not often find that in history ; you find it very seldom in the history of the Jews. Now and again, by the special decrees of Providence, some great prophet appoints, before his death, another great prophet to succeed him ; so Moses appoints Josue, and Elias appoints Eliseus. But as a rule the great figures of Old Testament history are solitary figures, and when they disappear there is nobody, or worse than nobody, to succeed them. The sons of Gedeon, one of the greatest of the Judges, the sons of the high priest Eli, the sons of the prophet Samuel, how soon they degenerated, and disgraced the traditions of their family ! But Mathathias, dying at the very outset of the campaign, leaves five sons. Of these, Eleazar is killed in the first important battle, but Judas is left in command ; only for a year or two, then he is killed in battle, and his brother John treacherously slain. Jonathan succeeds, and for eight years keeps the enemies of religion at bay. At last he is caught in an ambush ; but there is still one left ; Simon, the last of the brothers, eclipses the triumphs of his predecessors, and during the eight years of his leadership the nation flourishes as it has never flourished since, I suppose, the time of King Solomon. One patriot with five sons to succeed him, and not a single weak link in the chain ; here is a rare accident of history.

And the next point is this, that before they could muster their forces, and dispute with the heathen the mastery of their native soil, it was necessary for them to take refuge in the hill country, in their native city of Modin. Mathathias cried with a loud voice, ' Everyone that hath zeal for the law and maintaineth the testament, let him follow me,' and he and his sons fled into the mountains, and left all that they had in the city. It was in those same mountains that David had taken refuge, when he fled from the persecution of King Saul ; and he has sung of those outlaw strongholds of his in words that still echo through the sanctuaries of Christendom ; ' I will lift up mine eyes to the hills, whence cometh my help,' ' the Lord hath brought me out, and set me up upon a rock of stone '—the Machabees took him for their model, and retired to the hill fastnesses till they had gathered the strength needed for their effort.

And the third point is this ; that the Machabees did resolve to defeat the heathen with their own weapons. There was always a party among the Jews, at any moment of national crisis, which was for a non-resistance policy, what they called ' waiting on the Lord ; ' if God saw fit to deliver them, he would do so by a miracle ; no need, then, to oppose force with force. There were such men in the time of the Machabees ; and in particular there was a party of refugees which refused to fight on the Sabbath day, and was exterminated by massacre rather than break the letter of the Mosaic law by fighting on the day of rest. And we are told that the Machabees took, in view of that incident, a remarkable decision. ' Whosoever shall come against us to fight on the Sabbath day, we will fight against him, and we will not all die, as our brethren that were slain in the secret places.' If they were to do battle for the law of Moses, they must not press the letter of that law so as to imperil the whole success of their enterprise.

It is difficult for any English Catholic to read the two books of Machabees without being reminded of the situation in Europe four hundred years ago. It was, after all, the Renaissance, the rediscovery of the classical authors, and the return to classical models, which paved the way for the Continental Reformation ; it was the scepticism of the Greeks that infected the pure atmosphere of the Middle Ages, as it had infected, long before, the pure atmosphere of Jewish life. And the result, in our own country as in many others, was a profanation of holy places, a breaking down of altars, and carrying away of consecrated things ;

so that the very words of Scripture seem as if they had been written for our use. ' The Holy Places are come into the hands of strangers, her Temple is become as a man without honour ; the vessels of her glory are carried away captive. . . . Our sanctuary and our beauty and our glory is laid waste, and the Gentiles have defiled them.'

As the invasion of Antiochus had the effect of producing a reaction among the Jews, a return to stricter observance of the law and greater jealousy for the honour of the true God, so under the hand of Providence the apostasy of the sixteenth century produced, in Europe, that return to loyalty and that increase of Catholic zeal which we call the Counter-Reformation. And although St. Ignatius, when he founded the Company of Jesus, was not specially concerned to combat the errors of Luther, and turned his eyes rather to the Mohammedan world, at first, in his dreams of spiritual conquest, it is clear to us now that his Institute came just in time to put itself at the head of the Counter-Reformation movement, and save Europe for the faith. I hope you will not think me fanciful, then, Reverend Fathers, if I see in the Machabean brethren a type of that little Company of free-lances with which your holy founder defied the forces of his age, and fought with cheerfulness the battle of Israel.

I said that the Machabees, unlike other Jewish patriots, had the advantage of being a series ; their greatness did not die with Mathathias, or with Judas, or with Jonathan. So your Order is distinguished, I think, among the religious orders by the permanence of its tradition and its unfailing output of sanctity. From the year 1491 to the year 1716 there was never a moment at which there was not a Jesuit Saint alive on earth. I mean by Saints only such as have, by now,

been canonized by the Church ; is there any other
order, I wonder, that could make a similar boast ?
And what you can say of actual sanctity, you can say
also of the spirit of the Order. The Society of Jesus
has not, like other institutes, its periods of revival and
its periods of decay ; it retains, beyond precedent, the
memory of its first fervour. Where men complain of it,
they complain not of its relaxation, but of its activity ;
it has been suppressed, but it has never been reformed.
Let us thank God for that first, this unintermittent
spiritual energy which has marked the history of the
Society for four hundred years.

I said that the Machabees, as the condition of their
successful resistance, had first of all to withdraw into
the mountains and rally their forces there. ' He and
his sons fled into the mountains, and left all that they
had in the city '—it is surely, under Providence, the
long and careful novitiate of the Order, with the spirit
of detachment it produces, that has kept the spirit of
St. Ignatius alive. Other institutes have encouraged
retirement from the world, and access to the mountain-
life of contemplation, as an end in itself ; they have
exiled themselves from the corruptions of the world.
With the sons of St. Ignatius it is otherwise ; they have
retired to those mountains that they might swoop
down all the more successfully on the world they seemed
to have abandoned, and conquer it with the impetus of
their descent. Men have talked and written foolishly
as if the strength of the Society lay in its guardianship
of a secret, a secret oath, or a code of secret instructions,
or something of that kind. But it is not so ; the path
by which it guards its mountain stronghold is not a
secret path, but one plain to view, discouraging access
only by its steepness and ruggedness ; it is called
' The Spiritual Exercises.' The secret of the Order
is a secret which it has been giving away, century

after century, to anyone who will try its efficacy for himself.

I said that the Machabees determined to meet the world with its own weapons ; that they abandoned the policy of non-resistance which some of their partisans would have maintained, would not even be bound, in case of hostile attack, by the prescriptions of the Mosaic law which defined the Sabbath rest. They realized that armies trained under the Macedonian discipline could not be kept at bay by the same methods which had repelled, in time gone by, attack from the barbarians of the desert. And that, surely, is the astounding thing about St. Ignatius, if you view his influence on history merely from its human side. Long ago, when I was a Protestant, I remember playing some after-dinner game in which you were expected to write down the names of the six greatest men—I I think it was—in history, and surprising my company by including St. Ignatius' name among the list. When you read the beginning of his story, you are impressed with the feeling that you have here a thoroughly unpractical man ; the last, you might say, of the knights-errant. He was saturated himself, like Don Quixote, in the adventurous romances of his period, and he has developed, as the result, a Quixotic habit of mind. He will pursue and kill the Moor who has blasphemed our Lady—no, on second thoughts, he will give his horse its reins and see which path it takes. He will go out to the Holy Land and convert the Turks ; he will dress oddly to make the street-boys laugh at him—oh, a generous character, a lovable character, who will possibly do great things, but will he leave behind him any permanent legacy to be remembered by ? And then, all of a sudden, you find that this last of the knights-errant has turned into the first of the great business men. He has developed, heaven only knows how, capacities for organization which might have enabled him to name his own salary as the director of any modern enterprise ; he can make the world his chess-board.

He saw—not, surely, by any natural light—that the old fabric of Christendom was breaking up around him ; and that, in the troublous days which followed, the Church would need a body of free-lances, not specializing in one department or following one way of life, but ready to adapt themselves to any environment, to take up any form of legitimate activity, to go anywhere and do anything for the greater glory of God. And all that would need a spirit of obedience for which the existing religious Orders, with their carefully defined spheres of activity, were unsuited. A flying column of picked troops, throwing themselves into all the multifarious life of the modern world, yet always with the glory of God before their eyes. All the world's caricatures of Jesuit aims and Jesuit methods, all its cant use of the very word Jesuit, are a kind of distorted compliment. The modern world knows that the Society is a match for it, and takes its revenge in abuse.

I have left myself little time to draw a moral from all this for us others. Let us propose to ourselves a lesson of warning. When the Machabean brethren were at the height of their success, Joseph the son of Zacharias, and Azarias captain of the soldiers, said, ' Let us also get us a name, and let us fight with the Gentiles that are round about us ' ; they were routed and put to flight, because, says the sacred author, ' they did not hearken to Judas and his brethren, thinking that they should do manfully ; but they were not of the seed of those men by whom salvation was brought to Israel.' How easy it is to excuse ourselves for mingling freely in all society and in all pursuits of the world around us, thinking that we will be all the more effective Christians for being thorough men of the world ; how easy it is for us to get the worst of that encounter, and lose our standards, and be dragged down to the world's own level, if we are not of the seed of those men by whom salvation is to be brought to the Church ! Before we can do any good in the world or to the world, we must go up to the mountains and learn to separate ourselves from the world ; for us, as for the sons of St. Ignatius, the preface to any victory must be a retreat. The Saint whom we celebrate to-day bequeathed, not only to his own institute but to Christendom in general, one legacy for which, even if he had left no Order behind him, Christendom would owe him eternal gratitude—the Spiritual Exercises. It is generally so hard to imagine, ' What advice would such and such a Saint give to me, if I could meet him nowadays in the flesh ? ' ;   and, if our imagination can supply us with the answer, so hard to find how we, in our circumstances, can apply just that advice to ourselves.   But with St. Ignatius it is quite simple. Roughly speaking, you may say there was only one piece of advice he ever gave to anybody, and that was, ' Go into retreat.' He cries to us still, like Mathathias of old, ' Everyone that hath a zeal for the law, and maintaineth the Testament, let him follow me ' ; for our age, more than ever, that message holds good, if we are to save the world, if we are to save our souls.

XIV. ST. PHILIP NERI

(Preached at Birmingham, to the Oratory School.)

We are fools for Christ's sake. 1 *Corinthians* iv, 10.

IN uttering the praises of the Saints, it is possible to
concentrate your whole attention on the few features
of character that seem to be dominating, essential
features, and rule out of your considerations all that is
second and subsidiary to these as of no real importance.
In doing so, you assure yourself of an excellent moral ;
the only thing is that the farther you proceed the more
conscious you become that your Saint is beginning to
look exactly like everybody else's Saint—the same
mortifications, the same abandonment of love, the same
gifts in prayer. And at the end of your task you have
little left but a panegyric of St. N., which you can
easily use for St. Gregory the Great one week and Saint
Margaret Mary the next. Now, if such a study be your
aim, there could be no Saint who satisfied more
minutely all the tests of holiness than St. Philip. If
an outside enquirer wanted a book which would explain
to him what sort of person you meant by a Saint, you
certainly could not do better than refer him to Father
Bacci. But there is about St. Philip something so
personal, so intimate, so encouraging of familiarity,
that devotion in his case runs away from common
themes and edifying generalizations, and claims the
right to busy itself rather with what was singular and
characteristic about him than with the vital secret of
his sanctity.

I do not mean simply his extraordinary humanness.
It is quite true ; his figure stands out to us, after all

these centuries, as something very near and very natural
to us. He is ' the Saint of gentleness and kindness ' ;
' love is his bond, he knows no other fetter, asks not
our all, but takes whate'er we spare him ' : whatever
difference of temperament there might be, the greatest
of his English sons has not misinterpreted him. He is
fond of animals. He likes to have boys around him, and
does not mind how much noise they make if he can keep
them from sin—a mortification which, perhaps, it takes
a schoolmaster to appreciate. He fishes for souls with
the line, not merely with the net ; each penitent is, to
him, an individual soul to be wooed and won, not a
fresh case to be pigeon-holed. His portraits let you
see him ; nay, you can almost hear the cheerful ' What's
up ? What's up ? ' with which he greets his company.
I suppose the simplest way of putting it into a phrase
is to say that if you were alone in your room and the
door opened and one of the Saints walked in, if it were
almost any other you would fall on your knees, but if
it were St. Philip you would run to his heart.

But there is one special element in that humanness
which marks out Philip still more clearly from his
heavenly compatriots : I mean his fun. You hear in
the Middle Ages of God's minstrels or our Lady's
troubadours, but I think it was left for the Counter-
Reformation to produce that still more startling com-
bination, God's jesters. We have one of them, thank
God, in England, St. Thomas More. There was
nothing pleased him so much as the reflection that if
you put his name into Greek it meant a fool. He was,
perhaps, the only Saint who kept a private jester as an
honoured, almost a reverenced member of his house-
hold. He carried off his sanctity (which, surely, was
there long before he won his crown by martyrdom)
in a cloud of raillery, and went to the scaffold joking,
not like a man who has screwed himself up to it, but

like a man bubbling over with irrepressible amusement.
And St. Philip has, as we all know, something of this
same character. I do not mean his delightful habit of
self-depreciation, in which he has few parallels except,
perhaps, the Curé d'Ars. No, I mean that real, rollick-
ing fun of St. Thomas More, effervescing, in our
Saint, in the form of the most reckless practical jokes,
played, now on himself, now on his spiritual children.
There is no denying it, is there ? Why, one of the first
fathers of the Oratory confessed to having wondered
whether St. Philip were not touched in the head, and
St. Philip, in one of his most glorious flights of holy
fooling, made the poor man confess it in refectory.
No, we cannot get out of it, it is certainly there ;
St. Philip is always dancing in public, or changing
hats with somebody, or making his penitents put
their coats on inside out ; the fact cannot be
disputed.

And of course we all know—our aunts, I suppose,
did not let us forget it when we were small—that
the laughter of fools is like the crackling of thorns
under a pot, and a loud laugh betrays an empty
mind. Laughter, it is quite true, is a difficult thing
to find a warrant for in Scripture. It is quite true
that St. Philip always joked in public and because
he was in public ; quite true that his jokes always
produced a holy fruit of mortification. In a full
church, he went up to the Suisse or beadle at the
church door and pulled his beard. I suppose none
of us, in entering a foreign cathedral, can fail to be
conscious of a temptation to do that : the point
is that we are restrained by the fear of looking fools
and the fear of hurting the beadle's feelings—precisely
the two reasons why St. Philip did it. He succeeded
in making the bystanders think the worse of him,
and I suppose he succeeded in inflicting a **salutary**

mortification on the beadle, though Father Bacci, to the annoyance of his readers, does not say what followed. But the laughter was there, and if it had not been there would have been no mortification ; if everybody had kept his face who would have minded ? I do not suppose St. Philip pulled the beard really hard. No, St. Philip really believed in ragging, and believed in it as a means to attaining the salvation of souls.

And I do not think it is any good saying that this was part of Philip's natural temperament, which came out in spite of his sanctity. I find no evidence for that ; his early years are much like those of other Saints. No, it is a part of his sanctity ; somehow, in those long vigils at the Catacombs, he had found out a secret ; and that secret, for all his wonderful gift of tears, for all the miraculous palpitation of a heart love-sick for God, was one that could at times be communicated, could at times best be communicated to others, as a kind of celestial joke. The Holy Innocents, you would think, had been whispering in his ear. And he proceeded, not with a deep, artificial design, but, as St. Philip did everything, with complete naturalness and spontaneity, to make a fool of himself for Christ's sake.

Of course, if you were to ask which was nearer to the Saint's real interior life, his gift of tears or his gift of laughter, no one could hesitate in answering that it was his gift of tears. But the gift of tears is one which God, in his mercy, has granted to many others ; the laughter is a more special feature, a more isolated characteristic. Will it, then, be a waste of time to try and see what it was that gave the edge to Philip's sense of merriment as he moved about in this valley of Divine chastisement and of human tears ? I do not say that we shall be able to see the joke, if I may put it in that way; but it might be good for us even to understand what it was.

I say it may be hard for us to see it, because after all it is a joke against you and me and the world in general, and it is not always easy to see a joke when it is against yourself. There is, I suppose, no form of the ridiculous which has such a direct appeal as a situation in which somebody is putting on dignified airs, and all the time there is some circumstance, unknown to him but clearly seen by his audience, which makes that dignity absurd. You have come down without a tie, or somebody has written DONKEY on your back ; and not only is your dignity unavailing but actually, the more dignity you assume, the more irresistibly funny you look—to those who can see. Now, the Saint who has been with God, who has familiarized himself with the thought of God's greatness and the heavenly scale of values—what must he think when he comes back to the unreal pomps, the sordid competition, the pretentious would-be wisdom of the world's citizens? Must not he see man as a coxcomb, strutting about in borrowed plumes, and making himself ridiculous afresh with every fresh air he puts on of proprietorship or of self-assertion? Must not he see the world's mad competition as a fond striving for prizes not worth the dust of conflict, and only capable of deluding us because we never rest satisfied with their attainment, but press on at once after others no less transitory? Oh, yes, I grant you, the cynic equally gets that point of view, but the cynic has only found the moral from the record of his own disappointments, and his heart is soured and warped, so that he may scourge the world with satire, but cannot save it from itself. But the Saint, the man whose heart is all on fire with desire for the salvation of his fellow-men, yet

reads in the world about him the pathetic story of
their misdirected effort : who sees the mockery of
man's boasting, the futility of his striving, yet knows
that Man, so ridiculous in his parade of earthly
circumstance, is really a prince, if he but knew it,
only not here—will not he be privileged to greet
man's follies with the kindly laughter which has in
it an echo of heaven and, with the infectiousness of
that laughter, teach Man to know his present littleness, and through his littleness the greatness that
might be his ?

Sanctity, St. Philip used to say, rests within the
compass of three inches ; and he would point to his
forehead to shew that what he meant was the mortification of the *razionale*, the proper pride that is
perfection's most fatal enemy. And he knew that
if he could get a penitent to laugh at himself—
especially if worldly circumstances made it natural
for him to think too highly of himself—that laugh,
under God's Providence, would be the salvation of
his soul. And he knew that there was one man who,
but for God's grace, was in hourly danger of falling
into a fatal self-satisfaction over the greatness of the
revelations vouchsafed to him, and that man was
Philip Neri—very well, then, Philip Neri must be
relentlessly pursued with ridicule, must not pass a
day without being made to look silly. Yes, of course
there was the need of edifying others, but . . . of the
people that come to be edified, how large a proportion
are really in earnest, how many are merely sight-
seeing ? Some Polish nobles to see him ? No, they
are not really wanting to be edified ; come on, down
with the detective-stories, and let us be found reading
them to one another. . . . How like St. Philip ! And,
if I may be pardoned for saying so, how Oratorian !

But, you will say, you have not recommended any of

his virtues to our imitation, for surely this playfulness of his is the last thing we can afford to copy. No, I am not suggesting ways in which we could imitate St. Philip, but I think there is a quite practical lesson for our own advancement. Suppose you went into one of these Confessionals, and found the Saint himself sitting there ; suppose that, won over by that invitation so few could resist, you opened to him (if he had not opened it already to you) your whole heart—try to think what advice he would give. What humiliating penance would he impose ? In what strange garb would he make you walk through the streets of Birmingham ? What cherished calculations of self-interest would he dispel with that patient, insistent question : 'Yes, and then . . . ?' 'Yes, and then . . . ?' They are not distant historical figures, these Massimis and Tarugis you read of in the life ; they are men of the same fashion with us, with our temptations, our difficulties. Can we not learn to read in their story the needs of our own souls ?

Reverend Fathers, you cannot keep St. Philip to yourselves. The plant of devotion which seemed so exotic when first you imported it into England from beneath Italian skies, has become acclimatized to our northern region, and springs self-sown in our hedgerows. He sees, I do not doubt, other temptations in our hearts beyond what he read in the hearts of his own penitents, but surely none that his example cannot arm us against, or his prayers cannot remedy. May those prayers bring health to us who here celebrate his memory, and to all our countrymen, however little they have felt that influence till now, the graces they need for their eternal salvation.

XV. ST. CHARLES BORROMEO
(Preached at St. Mary of the Angels', Bayswater.)

A great tempest arose in the sea, so that the boat was covered with waves : but he was asleep. *Matthew* viii, 24.

IT is a common way of speaking in the Old Testament Scriptures to describe Almighty God as sleeping and awaking from sleep. When Israel is at the mercy of its enemies, and prayer and sacrifice is vain, when there is no voice and no answer of any that regards, then, by a natural metaphor, the Jew tells himself that God is asleep. He watching over Israel slumbers not, nor sleeps—that is the habitual confidence of Israel's faith. But when persecution arises, that confidence begins to vanish : ' Awake, Lord, why sleepest thou ? Awake, and be not absent from us for ever ' ; and when deliverance comes, ' the Lord awaked as one out of sleep.' And you will find that in some of our Lord's parables Almighty God is compared to a householder who slept—it is the same idea : wickedness flourishes on the earth, and Divine Providence seems to take no notice, seems unwilling to interfere. So I imagine that when our Lord's Apostles came to look back upon that terrible night in the Lake of Galilee, when they strained every nerve against the tempest while their Master lay sleeping in the boat, they found in it an allegory of their own situation, as they launched out the frail bark of his Church upon waves so troubled, with prospects so uncertain. And in every age the Church has looked back to that picture and taken comfort from it in times of adversity : ' Yes, our Master seems to sleep ; he gives no sign, vouchsafes

no apparent answer to our prayers : no matter, we
are safe from shipwreck, for he is still in our midst.'

When Julius Cæsar wished to cross from Durazzo to
Brindisi in a little boat, and the master of it wanted
to turn back, because the wind had risen and he was
in danger of shipwreck, Cæsar rebuked him for his
cowardice in noble words that have come down to us :
'Take courage, my friend, take courage, and fear
nothing ; Cæsar is your passenger, and Cæsar's
fortunes are your freight.' With greater, and with
better grounded confidence, the Church of God, which
is Peter's boat, has breasted the waves all through her
troubled history. It is not upon the captain's judgement or the pilot's experience, not upon human
wisdom or human prudence, that she depends for her
safe voyage : she rests secure in the presence of her
inviolable passenger. Yet we should do ill if we grudged
recognition and gratitude to those servants of his who
at various times have steered our course for us through
difficult waters, and especially to the Saints of the
Counter-Reformation — that remarkable group of
Saints whom God raised up at the time of Europe's
apostasy, by whose influence, humanly speaking, the
faith survived that terrible ordeal. And not the least,
nor the least prominent, of these is your holy patron,
who ruled the Church of Milan in the latter part of the
sixteenth century.

Say what you will, Italy breeds the genius for
government. So the greatest of Latin poets saw, and
summed it up for us in a phrase :

> Others shall quicken bronze with softer grace,
> And from dull marble life's own features trace ;
> Plead with more eloquence, the changing skies
> Map with more skill, and con the stars that rise :
> Roman, not these thy arts ;—thy agelong skill
> To wield thy empire o'er the peoples still.

Anybody, in naming the world's great men, will give you almost at once the names of two Italians, Julius Cæsar and Napoleon. And, whatever verdict history may pass on our own times, it is in Italy that the anarchical tendencies of the last half-century have provoked the first reaction in favour of efficient government. St. Charles came from a ruling family among that ruling race. Personal humility shone out in him as in the other Saints ; but there was something Latin all the same about the resolute competence with which he governed his diocese. Men called him a second St. Ambrose ; and St. Ambrose, his predecessor in the See of Milan, was a civil magistrate before he was ever a bishop. It was no idle title to call St. Charles a prince of the Church.

Whatever be the rights and wrongs of all the controversies we hear about the medieval Church, this at least is clear, that in the days of the Council of Trent its organization needed reform. And reform needs more than mere legislation to decree it ; it needs administration to execute it. That is St. Charles' characteristic legacy to the Church : it was the influence of his example, in great measure, that moulded her organization on the new model which Trent had decreed. The bishop has got to be the centre of everything in his diocese, and the clergy of the diocese are to be *his* clergy—a family of which he is to be the father, a guild of which he is to be the master. See how fond St. Charles was of synods : the whole of his comparatively short episcopate is a long record of the synods he gathered amongst his clergy. See how enthusiastic he is for the seminary idea ; the bishop, henceforth, is not merely to ordain people, he is to know whom he is ordaining. And above all what was characteristic of St. Charles was the institute which he left behind him—a body of

secular priests, putting themselves at the disposal of
the bishop as absolutely as the religious puts himself at
the disposal of his superior. Yes, there is much
about St. Charles' life which is more exciting, and
much which is more attractive, than all this ; his
boundless generosity to the poor, the relentless mortification that regulated his busy, competent life. But
what makes him stand out among the Saints more
than either is his intense devotion even to the most
uninspiring details of diocesan routine.

In this church, where St. Charles' own spiritual
children minister to you, something of his influence
must surely impart itself to you ; there must be some
response in your blood to the appeal, long strange to
our countrymen, of ' the Roman line, the Roman
order.' And it is only right that the faithful who
worship here should have a special devotion to
ecclesiastical authority, and to the expression of that
principle in the archdiocese of Westminster. It is the
aim of a decent Catholic to obey his superiors ; it is
the aim of a good Catholic to obey his superiors lovingly.
The virtue of obedience, nowadays, is a specifically
Catholic virtue. The Protestant or half-believing or
unbelieving world around us does not understand that
it is a virtue at all. English people by temperament,
by habit, by tradition, regard obedience as a tiresome
necessity. Useful as training, perhaps, for schoolboys
or for soldiers, but not a virtue in itself. The Protestant,
in fact, thinks that obedience exists because without it
there could be no authority. The Catholic is more
likely to tell you that authority exists because without
it there would be no obedience. The Catholic admits,
quite as much as the Protestant, that man ought to
realize himself, to develop every side of his nature, as
far as he can do so without sin. But he sees also that
the faculty for paying cheerful obedience to the orders

of a human superior is one side of a man's nature, and if he never recognizes a human superior, that faculty will go undeveloped. It is a good thing, says the Imitation, to be under obedience to a prelate, and not to be one's own master—a good thing, not a convenient thing or a necessary thing, but something good in itself, a source of merit.

You see, when your Protestant sits down, if he ever does, to read the biography of a man like St. Charles, he says : ' Ah, yes, that is where these Catholics have the advantage ! These crafty ecclesiastical statesmen, who treat every human agent they employ merely as a pawn in the game, who always sees exactly what each man is fitted for, and where he will be most use, that is where the power of the Catholic Church lies ! The Vatican issuing its orders to the bishop, and the bishops to their clergy, every one of whom is simply a cog in a great machine ! These seminaries, of course, turn all the priests out on a mould, and when they come out of them the bishop can play his crafty game of chess with them, and the thing is done. A triumph of organization, but hardly suited to the English mind or to modern circumstances.' That is the sort of picture of the Church which our obliging neighbours have invented for themselves in order to explain the fact that the Catholic Church is successful. We know that is a fable : we know that you have only got to live in the Catholic Church for a little in order to get the atmosphere of it, which is something totally different from that. But the Protestants are right about one thing ; they are right in seeing that we have a tradition and a theory of obedience which they do not understand. Only it is not the obedience of blind tools that have lost all independence and all initiative. It is a submissiveness which we imitate from our Lady herself—*Ecce ancilla Domini !* It is a free act of loyalty by which Catholics acknowledge and accept the administrative authority of the Church, and hear in the commands of their superiors the voice of Almighty God.

And above all, Catholic obedience rallies to the person of that Supreme Pontiff, who holds his succession from the Pilot of the Galilean lake. With good omen, in these troubled times, we have seen a successor of St. Charles in Milan elevated to the throne of St. Pius the Fifth. In the present disintegration of Europe, that recalls to Catholic memory the storms of the sixteenth century, yet with cross-winds and cross-currents that are all its own, let us pray that the spirit of those two great Saints may unite in their successor, as he grasps the tiller of Peter's boat, and finds, God be thanked, that she still answers her helm. And let us renew our own loyalty to his person and to his office, determined that those instruments of Government which the Saints of the Counter-Reformation perfected, shall not through our fault lose their edge or be baulked of their purpose, the glory of Almighty God. To whom be praise and dominion for ever. Amen.

XVI. THE ENGLISH MARTYRS

(*Preached at Tyburn Convent.*)

They that upset the world are come hither also. *Acts* xvii, 6.

WE enter this evening upon the Feast of the Invention of the Holy Cross, and to-morrow its relics will be exposed for veneration all over the world. Did you ever reflect, as you knelt before

one of those chips of wood, upon its early history?
Its history, I mean, before it became the instrument
of our salvation. We have no record of its origin;
in what forest the tree grew, or for what end it was
first cut, or how it came to be brought to Jerusalem.
Two planks, I suppose, lying about somewhere,
and a soldier, the handy man of the legion, would
fix them roughly together; not quite straight, perhaps, not quite true, but 'after all,' he would say
to himself, 'it is good enough for what it has got
to do.' A careless piece of carpentry, one of three
jobs that had to be done by next morning, and in
a hurry, because the need for it was unforeseen.
And to-morrow a mere splinter of that wood, such
as a man might run into his hand, will draw thousands
of worshippers to their knees.

It is curious, is it not? Yet hardly more curious
than the collection that is kept in this building;
fragments of human bones and hair, patches of coarse
cloth, shreds of linen with some dark stain on it. . . .
Can you imagine what a stranger from some other
planet would make of it, a man, if such were possible,
without any idea or conception of God? You would
persuade him that the collection was not one of
mere odds and ends; that a certain interest attached
to these things merely from the historical fact of
their having been in contact with men of times past,
the victims of a series of judicial murders. 'Yes,'
he would say, 'but, even so, is it not rather morbid?
Is not one Chamber of Horrors enough for you people
in London? Surely it is a perverted instinct in our
nature that makes a story of crime so thrilling to us,
that brings out a crowd on a cold morning just to
see a flag hoisted when some murderer in a prison
forfeits to justice the life he has misused; that throngs
the inquest, and hardly allows the ambulance to

pass ? Is it well to feed this unnatural taste by keeping
alive in perpetuity the trophies of a tyranny that
has long since passed ? ' And we should try to tell
him about the martyrs, and what they mean to us.
And he would still persist : ' Yes, but are you not
making much of that very thing of which the martyrs
themselves made so light ? They handed over their
bodies to the tormentor precisely because their bodies
were of no account in comparison to their immortal
souls ; and you, in your ghoulish treasure-chambers,
hoard up the very trappings of mortality they despised.
Did not St. Thomas More, as you call him, move his
beard aside from the block because *that* had not
committed treason ? The soul, surely, not the body,
is what matters. Cannot you bury the bodies of your
Saints in peace, and be content that their name
should live for evermore ? '

What answer should we make ? I suppose this :
That we do not treasure these relics as men treasure
the ghastly evidences of some atrocious crime, but
rather as the trophies of a conquest ; we gather these
bones as you might gather the droppings of some
precious metal that had been tried in the fire, we
catch the drops of blood as if it were some rare vintage
flowing from the wine-press. If a housebreaker
gave us the choice whether he should steal one of
these bones, or the golden reliquary that enshrines
it, we should, without affectation, resign the reliquary
as a thing of smaller worth. We put a different value
on these historical events from those around us.
These men, you see, were the men who upset the
world. And for us, their children, the world is still
topsy-turvy, and the meaning of things and the values
of things are stated, for us, in terms of a new currency.
To us death is life, and defeat is victory. I love that
phrase, used of the Apostles, ' these men that upset

the world '—so much so, I am afraid, that I have
taken the liberty of translating it as it stands in the
Greek original, although the present text of our
Latin Bible, by an obvious slip which I have no doubt
the Pontifical Commission will set right, has represented St. Jerome as writing Urbem, the city, instead
of Orbem, the world. To upset the world—it is
the word that's used to describe the depopulating
of a conquered country, when the victor turns everybody out of house and home and pulls down their
roof-trees about their ears. The martyrs are the
people who have done that to the whole world.
Whenever we feel inclined to turn round and settle
down and feel really comfortable in this world of
our pilgrimage, the example of the martyrs is there
to evict us and make us feel uncomfortable once more.
God's Saints don't content themselves with overcoming the world, they are determined to make the
place quite uninhabitable for you and me. That
is the boast of our religion ; it's also the reason why
some people dislike it.

But I am going ahead too fast ; let us tell our
strange visitor who these martyrs were and what
were the circumstances of this deplorable miscarriage
of justice. The question which sent St. Thomas
More and St. John Fisher, whom we commemorate
especially at this time, to their deaths, was the question
whether they would take or refuse an oath which
recognized the validity of an adulterous union con-
tracted by their sovereign ; the preamble to which
oath—only the preamble—cast aspersions on the
right of the Holy See to judge (as it did judge, in
a contrary sense) matters of this character. This
was long before any considerable body of people
in England had contemplated the possibility of
being anything other than Catholics. To the mass

of men, even to devoted Catholics, even to the martyrs'
best friends and kinsmen, the refusal of the oath
seemed a scruple, an exaggeration of conscience.
Could not a man take the oath without committing
himself to all the bad doctrine that might be contained in the preamble ? Was it even wise to force
an issue between the monarchy and the Papacy ?
Do not let us blame the people who argued like that.
They could not see, as we can see now, what this
defiance of ecclesiastical authority was to lead to.
The Chancellor, in criticizing St. Thomas More's
conduct, said it reminded him of a fable of Æsop
about a country where it was prophesied that a strange
rain was about to fall, which would turn everybody
it wetted into fools. All the wisest men hid themselves
when it came, and expected afterwards to be able
to have the fools at their mercy, but found instead
that the fools persisted in governing themselves
their own way, and they would have been wiser
still to stay out in the rain and be turned into fools
like the rest of them. It was true ; the minds of
the generality of men had been blinded, and the
few wise men who had escaped that infection must
either resign their sane opinions or pay for them
with their lives.

But there were such people. The upsetters of
the world had come hither also ; had come even
to England, to upset things just when everybody
was going to be comfortable. They had that awkward,
subversive temperament which sees everything upside
down, which measures life only as the ante-chamber
of death, time only as the preface to eternity. St.
Thomas More really could not see that he was any
worse off in the Tower than at Chelsea ; they were
both equally close to heaven. And yet this was a
man to whom his home was a sort of Paradise, who

would have been unwilling, you would think, to spend a day out of reach of his library! He has learned, somehow, to measure things by the standard of eternity, and the peace of his own soul really does mean more to him than the peace of his country. He deliberately breaks up our home, our comfortable home, the world.

We do not forget, and God forbid that we should forget, the cause for which our martyrs died. Because the faith for which they suffered persecution was their faith in the privileges divinely conferred upon the Holy See, it is for us, their clients and their fellow-countrymen, to be distinguished, if there must be such distinction, above the other nations of the world by our whole-hearted devotion to the Vicar of Christ. So much is due in expiation for the sins of our fore-fathers, in gratitude for the testimony borne by our holy patrons. But it is not for us to perpetuate by letting the grim memories of past wrongs rankle in our minds, our personal quarrel with the Protestantism which sent the martyrs to their death. Bear a grudge against the Church of England for events that happened nearly four centuries ago? Believe me, it would be an unnecessary compliment. For the Church which—in some of its utterances—claims continuity with the Christendom of Augustine and Dunstan, cannot even claim the credit of continuity with itself. The Christianity which we see around us has little to do, for better or for worse, with the Christianity of the sixteenth century divines. Brought up in the breezy historical tradition of Charles Kingsley and the smaller Gardiner, it leaves the record of the martyrs a forgotten page in history. Well, in the face of that forgetfulness, it is good indeed that we should do everything to tend the memory of our martyrs, and to make public display of our devotion, but it should be with no feelings of resentment towards the mutilated Christianity which the evil tradition of the persecutors has left to our fellow-countrymen. For, after all, what the martyrs triumph over is not the fury of the persecutor, it is the spell of the things which persecution takes from them : they triumph over the attractiveness of peace, of ease, of liberty, of comfort, of companionship, of health, and finally —the greatest attraction of all—of life itself. You do not tremble, when you read the story of St. Thomas More confronting his judges, lest he should be brow-beaten or bullied into surrender. But you do catch your breath just a little for fear heaven should lose a martyr, when wife and daughter, not of any ill intent, but with misplaced affection, come to dissuade him from his holy purpose. A smaller man might have resisted the efforts of a Cromwell ; it needed the martyr's heroism to resist the appeals of Margaret Roper. If we are to learn to imitate St. Thomas More, we shall not do it by despising Protestants ; we shall do it by despising Chelsea. It is the world that the martyrs trample under their feet ; it is the world they would have us triumph over as best we may.

Of this attitude of defiance towards the world our English Catholicism ought, from the very circumstances of its past, to be a continual reminder. It is a matter of historical atmospheres. To have had the experience of teaching—if you will pardon my being autobiographical—in an Oxford College founded by Sir Thomas Pope, who was actually St. Thomas More's gaoler in the Tower ; to have gone on to teach at a school which acknowledged as its chief benefactors King Edward the Sixth and Queen Elizabeth ; and then, as a Catholic, to find yourself teaching at the very college founded by an exiled

Cardinal for the training of seminary priests for
England in the time of the persecution—that change
means, so far as your historical perspective is concerned, a complete change of values. To have been
brought up among the busts of portly gentlemen
in semi-classical costume who became Lord Chan-
cellors and Poets Laureate and what not, people
who started as boys with your hopes, your ambitions,
and succeeded, one way and another, in scrambling
up the difficult slopes of fame, among portraits of
Bishops with puffy sleeves and lawyers in important
wigs ; and then to find yourself in a place where the
most treasured roll of school successes is a long list
of names the world has never heard of, men who
died convicted as traitors to their country—that
should be, to anybody, a sufficiently impressive
sermon on the rewards to be sought in this world
and in the next. I was taught where, we are assured
on good authority, the battle of Waterloo was won.
I am teaching where the battle of Tyburn was won,
and I thank God for it.

Oh, how they upset the world for us, these martyrs
of ours, or if they do not, how they ought to upset
it for us ! Where we seek our gratification, they found
their mortification ; they blessed the discomforts
we repine at, spurned the crowns we pant for, flicked
their fingers at the master that so easily whistles us
to heel—human respect. To us, eternity is a mere
background, sketched in dimly behind this life, the
central incident on our mind's canvas. To them,
the picture was the landscape of eternity ; the figures
of this world were merely dotted about in the fore-
ground to give value to the rest. And at Tyburn,
whether it be the influence of their prayers or the
continuous miracle of the Eucharistic Presence, I
cannot say, but there is a spirit that communicates

to those who offer their prayers in this place something of that other worldly focus. The wheels hum and the motors hoot and the cries of the street fall on your ear, but, praying here before the monstrance, you know, somehow, that this, not that, is the reality, here, not there, is the true current of human endeavour. We, too, if only for the moment, feel that we could endure like the martyrs as seeing him who is invisible, that amidst the world's changefulness our hearts could there be set, where are the true joys. For a moment we really see the world as the puppet-show it is.

Let us praise God, then, for our English martyrs, Thomas More and John Fisher and the Charterhouse monks, and, from Blessed Cuthbert Mayne onward, the long line of proscribed and hunted priests. Men of our blood, they have left sayings which ring more familiarly to us than the translated pieties of the Continent ; men of our latter-day civilization, they stand out with more of human personality than the mist-wreathed heroes of the medieval world. And surely, if they have not forgotten among those delights of eternity the soft outlines and the close hedgerows and the little hills of the island that gave them birth ; if in contemplating the open face of God, they have not ceased to take thought for the well-loved kingdom that exiled and disowned them, the patiently evangelized people that condemned and hurried them to the gallows, their prayers still rise especially, among all the needs of a distracted world, for the souls we love whom error blinds or sin separates from God. It is Mary's month ; we hardly dare, so wide are the sympathies of her immaculate Heart, to think of our country as singled out in her intercessions : yet we are her dowry, and while the world lies suppliant at her feet she will not forget the triduum we keep in these first days of May. God grant that through the power of such intercessors, whatever unworthiness and degeneracy he sees in us English Catholics of a later day may be pardoned and set aside, and that our brethren, so long sought, so patiently wooed by the Divine grace, may return to the allegiance of the true Church, and make England a shrine of martyrs and a nursery of Saints once more.

XVII. THE OXFORD MARTYRS

(Preached at the Undergraduates' Chaplaincy.)

Remember the days of old ; think upon every generation. *Deuteronomy* xxxii, 7.

YOU will probably have seen in the papers this week, if you did not know it before, that the claim of some two hundred and fifty of our fellow-countrymen to the honours of martyrdom are now being considered at Rome ; and that a large number of them, some two hundred in all probability, are likely to be beatified either this month or in the very near future. By a fortunate accident, the feast of the Oxford martyrs, which we celebrate in this archdiocese, falls this year on a Sunday, this Sunday. The whole total of the English martyrs, if you include those who have already been beatified, is three hundred and fifteen ; and in view of the historical circumstances it is not a little remarkable that exactly one-fifth of these were Oxford men. No less than seventeen colleges are represented out of a possible twenty. It would be out of place, I think, to go over the old ground of controversy and remind ourselves once more how monstrous was the attempt of politicians, and later of historians, to brand the great majority (at least) of these names with the stigma of treason. Instead of that, I thought I would just give you a few thumb-nail biographies, if I may so call them, of a few among these many ; and I have chosen, for that purpose, the names of those Oxford men who have already been beatified, and who suffered as seminary priests in the earlier years of Queen Elizabeth's reign, before the Spanish Armada. This selection will reduce the whole number to a dozen or so ; we have hardly time for more.

You must begin any such list with the Jesuit, Blessed Edmund Campion. He was one of the original scholars of St. John's when it was founded in 1555 ; he became public orator of the university and junior proctor. He was generally regarded as *the* Oxford man of his period, and Queen Elizabeth herself was delighted with his eloquence. But of course he enjoyed all this fame under a miserable condition ; he had to take the oath of supremacy, and was ordained deacon according to the ritual of the Protestant Prayer-book. He thought, perhaps, as many have thought since his time, that he could do better work for the Catholic cause by ' staying where he was.' Like Newman, he exercised an extraordinary influence over the minds of others ; like Newman, he must have felt that his choice lay between Oxford and Rome. He left Oxford, and went over to Dublin, still as a Protestant ; but his conscience was being too strong for him, and after witnessing the trial of Blessed John Story in London he went abroad,

first to Douai, and then to Rome, where he entered
the society. He worked first in Bohemia ; then was
sent on the English mission, and, among other vast
apostolic labours, printed his ' Ten Reasons ' at a
secret printing press. He was apprehended at Lyford
Grange, near Wantage ; was offered life and preferment by the Queen herself if he would return to
Protestantism ; was mercilessly racked, and finally,
by an afterthought, condemned on a ridiculous charge
of treason. He suffered at Tyburn on this day, in the
year 1581.

St. John's also claims the first martyr among the
secular clergy, Blessed Cuthbert Mayne. He was
educated by his uncle, a priest who had conformed to
the new religion. He was apparently already ordained
when he came up, first to St. Alban's Hall—that is, for
practical purposes, to Merton—and then to St. John's,
where the took his M.A. in 1570. In the same year,
when he was already considering the question of his
religious allegiance, like other members of Campion's
circle, a letter addressed to him from abroad fell into
the wrong hands ; he disappeared from Oxford, and
we next meet him in 1573, at Douai, where he was
ordained, and sent back to England in 1576. He
worked in Cornwall, where he passed as the steward
of a well-to-do Catholic ; but after a year of this the
pursuivants found him, and he was led off to trial.
No charge was brought against him which could be
supposed to have any political bearing whatsoever.
One of the judges protested against his sentence, and
the case had to be remitted to London ; the Government simply ordered his execution, and he was
murdered on November 29, 1577.

When Sir William Petre extended the foundation of
Exeter in 1565, one of the first scholars he nominated
was Ralph Sherwin, who took his degree there in 1574,

and was reckoned an accomplished scholar both in Greek and in Hebrew. By the next year he, too, had left for Douai. Not much is known of his life, and he was apprehended when he had only been on the mission for about half a year. But the story of his imprisonment, of his twice-repeated torture on the rack, and of the five days during which he lay without food or drink, and found at the end of them 'no distemper in his joints by reason of his racking' are among the most noteworthy of our martyrs' records. He should also be remembered for some of his last utterances; it was he who, after his condemnation, pointed up at the sun and said: 'I shall soon be above yon fellow'; he who said on the scaffold: 'If to be a Catholic only be to be a traitor, then I am a traitor'; he who died with the words 'Jesu, Jesu, Jesu, esto mihi Jesus.' He was martyred at the same time as Blessed Edmund Campion.

In 1574 a strikingly handsome young man came up to Hert Hall, which we now call Hertford. His name was Alexander Briant; he came from Somersetshire, where the old faith had died hard. It was a Somersetshire man, Robert Persons, who was afterwards a member of the Society of Jesus and one of the most active, if not always one of the most discreet, partisans of the Catholic cause in England. Persons was then a fellow of Balliol, and young Briant was his pupil, so that he must have been early attracted towards the Catholic cause. He must have gone down without taking his degree, for by the year 1578 he had already gone out to Douai and been ordained priest there. He returned to England, and went back to his own county of Somerset, to reconcile heretics and minister to Catholics. Among others he reconciled the father of his old Oxford tutor. When he was apprehended, as he very soon was, he had to suffer for this connexion;

the Government were particularly anxious to lay hands on Persons, who was then himself in England, and they tortured Alexander Briant unmercifully in the hope of information, driving needles, for example, between his finger-nails and fingers. Soon before his martyrdom, he applied for and was granted admission into the Society of Jesus. He suffered with Campion and Sherwin, on this day, at the age of twenty-eight.

For myself, I feel specially bound to pray to Blessed Thomas Ford, fellow of Trinity in 1567. He was a Devonshire man, and perhaps as a Devonshire man he was already acquainted with Cuthbert Mayne at St. John's ; certainly it was he who warned Mayne of the danger threatening him when that letter from abroad went astray. Nor was it long before he himself followed his friend abroad, arriving at Douai in 1570. He took a long course at Douai, and did not come back to England till 1576 ; he was sent to work at Lyford Grange, not far from Abingdon—indeed, it is not a dozen miles from where we sit ; and it is clear that there were close relations between the Catholics who remained in Oxford, and the safe moated grange in Berkshire where they could go off to hear Mass. It was quite an establishment that Mrs. Yate kept there ; there were eight Bridgettine nuns sheltered in her house. Then one day there was great excitement in the little colony—Edmund Campion was to pay them a visit. He came, stayed the night, and left ; then Thomas Ford had to ride after him and bring him back, because a crowd of sixty or more, from Oxford and elsewhere, had come over to hear him preach. His return was fatal to him, and to Thomas Ford as well ; both of them, with another priest, were observed by a spy and captured in a hiding-place where they had taken refuge. So Thomas Ford shared the ignominious

ride to London with Campion, and Campion's imprisonment ; he was finally condemned on the accusa-
tion that he had taken part in a conspiracy, or an
alleged conspiracy, in Rome and again at Rheims,
during a time which he had, as a matter of fact, spent
entirely in England. He was martyred some time after
Campion, in 1582.

As Campion and Ford were being taken from Lyford
to London, they were passing through a part of the
country where the faith still had its strongholds,
notably at Stonor Hall, near Henley. It was at
Henley that another priest incautiously tried to speak
with Campion, so giving himself away and being
carried off with the others. This was William Filby,
an Oxford martyr in a double sense ; for he was a
native of the town, and had been up as an under-
graduate at Lincoln. He matriculated in 1575, and
was at Rheims by 1579 ; there he was ordained, and
must presumably have been sent to work in Oxford-
shire, but as he was only ordained in 1581, the year of
Campion's apprehension, he must have had a short
missionary life. From the November of that year till
the following May he was kept in handcuffs, and then
executed at Tyburn.

Two other Oxford priests were executed with him,
both from Brasenose. One of these, Laurence Richardson, was a Lancashire man, and not only came from
Lancashire, still so largely Catholic, but from Great
Crosby, still intimately connected with the name of a
Catholic family. It seems pretty clear that he must
have been a ' born Catholic,' as we say, and we may
perhaps look upon him as a member of this congregation in a sense in which Edmund Campion and the
others were not. Nevertheless he seems to have
managed to take his degree ; that was on November
25, 1573 ; and Challoner says that he was a fellow of

the College, though Gillow seems to deny this : the family from which he came were recusants right up to 1717, and it seems hard to understand how he could conscientiously have taken a fellowship under the religious conditions of those times. In any case, he left Oxford almost immediately for Douai, where he was admitted in 1573. He returned as a priest, four years later, to Lancashire, and acted as chaplain at Ince Blundell—the Blundells were his cousins. In Lancashire persecution was not so easy to organize as in the south, but he was apprehended in London, and charged with complicity in the same plot in which Thomas Ford was supposed to have been involved, though he too had never left England during the time in question. He was martyred in 1582, repeating St. Stephen's words : Lord Jesus receive my soul.

The other Brasenose man who was martyred at the same time was, like Laurence Richardson, a man of good family, and came like him from Lancashire. His brother, who succeeded to the estates, appears on the recusants' rolls, but he, it seems, must have been reconciled to the Church, for the parents were Protestants. Thomas Cottam, therefore, will have come up as a Protestant ; he took his degree in 1568, and then went off to teach at a grammar school in London. Here he was converted, and went abroad ; his desire was, apparently, to join the Society of Jesus and go out to the Indian missions. His health prevented this, and he was ordained at Rheims in 1580. The moment he landed at Dover he was arrested, on the evidence of a spy who had met him abroad. Then an extraordinary thing happened. The Mayor of Dover gave him into the charge of a gentleman who was travelling to London, to be delivered into safe custody there. This gentleman was really a Catholic and a priest,

Dr. Ely by name ; and he insisted on Thomas Cottam going free when he got to London, though somewhat against his own conscience.   Later, Dr. Ely was in danger of getting into trouble for not delivering up his prisoner, and Cottam voluntarily gave himself up to save the situation.   He was taken to the Marshalsea and tortured ; out of sheer wantonness, it would seem, because they did not try to extract any secrets from him.   He was thirty-three when he went to his eternal reward.

The same college produced another of these martyrs, John Shert.   He was a Cheshire man, and took his degree from Brasenose in 1566 ; like Cottam, he was for a time a schoolmaster in London, then went to Rheims, and came back to England in 1579.   His work lay in London, and there for two years he managed to escape detection ; he was then committed to the Tower, and condemned with Thomas Ford for the conspiracy which he, like Thomas Ford, knew nothing at all about ; he, too, had been in England at the time alleged.   He suffered immediately after Thomas Ford, to whom he boldly prayed on the scaffold as to one already in heaven.

Lincoln, too, has another beatified martyr, Blessed William Hart.   He came from Somersetshire and caught the infection of Catholicism which still lingered in Oxford ; went abroad to Douai and afterwards to Rome, and was ordained priest, it seems, when he was only twenty-one.   He worked on the mission at York, where his charity and his eloquence made him almost a public figure ; yet even in York, where sympathy with the old religion was still strong, he went in danger of his life, and on one occasion had to climb down the walls of the castle and hide in a moat to save his life. They arrested him on Christmas Day, 1582 ; and the charges at his trial were so frivolous that the foreman of the jury demanded to be dismissed, and had actually to be dismissed before a verdict was brought in against him. A most touching letter, written to his Protestant mother on the eve of his execution, has been preserved to us. He suffered in 1583.

Two months later, in the same city of York, they executed another Oxford martyr, Blessed Richard Thirkeld. He was up at Queen's in 1564–65, but it is not known what became of him between that time and his ordination at Rheims, fourteen years later. He was a native of Durham, and when he came back to England he was stationed at York, where he was confessor to the well-known martyr, Margaret Clitheroe. He was one of those martyrs who have longed for martyrdom from the first ; for eight years he had prayed for it. Accordingly, when he was arrested on York bridge and accused of being a priest, he immediately admitted it, instead of leaving it to his prosecutors to prove the charge. He actually appeared in court in his cassock and biretta ; and he was condemned without difficulty on his willing confession that he had reconciled the Queen's subjects to their allegiance to the spiritual power of the Pope. When he was executed, the Mayor of York held a general meeting of the citizens elsewhere, for enrolling the militia ; so doubtful was the effect, in York, of public executions for religion.

Well, there are eleven martyrs for you. I have not included two Oxford martyrs who suffered under Elizabeth, Blessed Thomas Plumtree of Corpus, and Blessed John Storey, master of Broadgates Hall (now Pembroke), because although they suffered under Elizabeth they were not seminary priests ; they had been brought up at Oxford when it was still a centre of Catholic learning, before the death of King Henry the Eighth. Remember that these names are only a fifth of those martyrs, beatified or waiting to be beatified, whom Oxford numbers among her sons ; remember that the Oxford martyrs in their turn have to be multiplied by five before you reach the total of the English martyrs.

I am not going to draw any elaborate morals from what I have told you. I would just draw your attention to the ages of these men ; I suppose their average age was about thirty-one ; they did not live long, and they knew that they would not live long. When they were up at Oxford the world was all at their feet, and a world which held out greater opportunities, one would say, than our world, for men who wanted to make a name and get the best out of life. They could hope to become paragons of chivalry like Sidney, courtiers like Raleigh, adventurers like Drake, poets like Spenser ; or, if they were determined to embrace a clerical career, there were easy openings for them, and ample emoluments for them, in the Church of England. But conscience beckoned them, and they gave up all that prospect, to go and live in a little dusty Flemish town, which promised them the life of an outlaw, and death at thirty-one.

They were our fellow-students ; as they lay in prison, little vignettes of Oxford must have danced before them ; the Cottages at Worcester, and Mob Quad at Merton, and Christ Church Hall, and Magdalen Tower, and New College cloisters, and the old library at Trinity, and the front of St. John's, were as familiar sights to them as to us who follow them ; they must remember them still, if heaven is to be the completion of our life on earth. St. Silvester, whose feast we celebrated last Tuesday, was converted by the sight of a young man's corpse in an open grave ; ' This man,' he said to himself, ' was what I am ; what this man is, I shall be.' Let us take a kindred lesson from the martyrs of whom we have been speaking. They were what you are, Oxford undergraduates. God grant that you may be what they are, citizens of the kingdom of heaven.

XVIII. THE DERBY MARTYRS

(Preached in the market square at Derby.)

For we are the good odour of Christ unto God, in them that are saved and in them that perish ; to the latter indeed the odour of death unto death, but to the former the odour of life unto life. 2 *Corinthians* ii, 15.

ON July 24, 1588, at a moment when the Spanish Armada was cruising off the south coast, somewhere between Plymouth and the Isle of Wight, three Catholic priests were put to death in this town with the horrible tortures then prescribed for those guilty of high treason. Their offence, as usual, was a merely technical one, that of being priests and of celebrating Mass ; there is no record which suggests that they had been concerned with political activities. The name of the best known among these three priests was Nicholas Garlick.

Garlick—it is not a pretty name. It reminds you, inevitably, of a class of plants with a very pungent smell, which most of us dislike. And I have no doubt that on that day of July, more than three hundred years ago, the street boys of Derby made merry on the subject, holding their noses, as likely as not, while Nicholas Garlick was drawn on his hurdle to the gallows. They will have thought of garlic as the name of a nasty scent ; they will have forgotten that this plant, however distressing it may be to the nostrils, has a high medicinal value. The smell of it may be deadly, but its properties are life-giving. If they had thought of that, their minds might perhaps have travelled back to another preacher of the Christian religion, fifteen centuries before ; they might have remembered how he wrote to his friends in Corinth : ' We are the good odour of Christ ; to them that perish, the odour of death unto death ; but to them that are saved, the odour of life unto life.'

An odour of death unto death, an odour of life unto life—that means that the Christian message is what you make of it. If you find it deadly, then it is deadly, to you ; if you find it life-giving, then it is life-giving, to you. I do not mean that at the time when our martyrs suffered, all those who took part in tormenting them, all those who joined in the cry against them and jested at them on their way to execution, involved themselves thereby in eternal damnation. The tendency to shout with the crowd is one of the strongest, and on the whole one of the most pardonable tendencies, in human nature ; nor can there be much doubt, I suppose, that at the time of the Spanish Armada the English public was worked up into an attitude of intense antipathy to everything which it suspected of being foreign. Fear is a great promoter of cruelty. But I do say that when you read the history of the martyrs you will find in it an admirable illustration of how the doctrines of our holy religion, which seem, and are, so life-giving to us, can seem, and be (so far as their rejection is culpable), deadly to those who reject them.

An odour of death—the Catholic religion had already begun to seem, to the young people of that day, a dead thing, a back number, a page from the history of the past. Human memories are lamentably short ; there must have been old folks in Derby who could remember the Old Religion well enough ; who had seen, when they were young, the habits of the black monks and the black nuns, and had experience of their charity. But the younger people—remember that the Protestant religion had been in the saddle for thirty years. The days of Queen Mary were exactly as remote from them as the days of Queen Victoria are from us. If you think of all the changes that have come over England since 1901 ; if you think, for example, of the growth of the Labour Movement in these thirty years, that will give you some idea of how remote the Catholic religion must have appeared to the people who were just growing up and marrying at the time of the Spanish Armada.

These priests, then, these seminary priests who slunk about the town in their disguises, must have seemed to Englishmen of the day part of a dead world, like ghosts from the old graveyards which housed the bones of their Catholic ancestors. And yet there must have been old-fashioned people about the town, with their families, who had never accepted the new religion ; had conformed to it outwardly, perhaps, through fear of consequences, but had never come to believe in the claims of the usurping ministers who occupied the parish pulpits. And to them, these seminary priests were an odour of life ; they brought back memories of the old days when Mass was said at St. Alkmund's, when the figures, the emblems of our Lady and the Saints were to be seen everywhere, in a brighter and a freer England. In this dead world of Protestantism the sight of Father Garlick or Father Ludham, passing by them without recognition in the street, was like a ray of sunshine piercing through fog. For these men brought with them that Bread of Life which had been interdicted to a starving England these thirty years. An odour of life unto life.

An odour of death—how they must have marvelled, those ordinary Englishmen of the day, at the persistency with which priest after priest came back from the Continent to work on the English mission, only to fall after a year or two into the hands of the pursuivants, and atone for their heroism by death! These three priests of whom we are speaking had only been able to work for souls half a dozen years before they met their end; and in each case with an interval of banishment. How mad they must have thought us, to suppose that we were going to keep alive the embers of the old religion, when a seminary course of six years only qualified our priests for six years of apostolate! If ours was not a dead religion, at least ours was a dying body; a few years more, and it would be bound to come to an end, from sheer attrition of numbers. Poor Garlick, only another weed rooted out, as all the weeds must before long be rooted out, from the beautiful, ordered garden of Protestant England!

And yet—an odour of life; those others, those few who still clung to the faith of their ancestors recognized, with whatever doubts, with whatever failings of the heart, that this long pageant of butchery, so far from threatening the Catholic religion with extinction, was in reality deepening and widening its influence; that every judicial murder meant another martyr praying before the throne of God for our apostate country, another model of fortitude, to encourage fresh souls to embrace the same hazardous career, another outrage, to sicken Englishmen at last of the brutal work. One after another, political hopes failed them; but they clung on, none the less jealously, to the tradition of their forefathers, and left a stock surviving to be fertilized in God's own time, and to grow and flourish beyond all the measure of their hopes.

Still doomed to death, and fated not to die—so wrote our Catholic poet of the faith he had embraced; and this has been, everywhere and at all times, its history. For it seems, our faith, a thing rooted in the past, wrapped up with a great deal of venerable imagery, of forgotten ceremony, of exploded tradition; so that even those who hate it will sometimes speak of it in tones of hushed respect, as men speak of the dead. But the fact is that it is alive; that in the midst of all this modern hurry and heedlessness of the past, all this frantic worship of to-morrow, our Church is attracting converts to itself as no other religious body in England is attracting them, is expanding its borders as no other religious body in England dares to expand them. It looked a dead thing compared with the Protestant religion which had superseded it, thirty years after Elizabeth came to the throne; to-day, thirty years after Queen Victoria ended her reign, does the same comparison survive? Is it not rather true that those who are frightened of us, and there are still many who are frightened of us, attribute those fears, openly, to the growth in Catholic numbers and Catholic influence which our generation has witnessed?

The Catholic Church always seems to despise all measures which would promote her own survival. She takes some of her most devout sons, and bids them follow, in the priesthood, a life of celibacy; she takes many of those women whom you would expect to become the mothers of pious Catholic families, and immures them in the cloister. You would say she was pursuing a policy of ecclesiastical race suicide. And yet in our own day, when parenthood has ceased to be held in honour, and thoughtful men are directing our attention to a decline in the birth-rate, and the possibility that the English stock will die out, it is the Catholic body more than any other which is resisting that tendency and breeding the Englishmen of the next generation. It is the odour of life, not of death, that breathes from the Catholic Church, now as then.

Only, now as then, we Catholics have to keep alive among us that same spirit of devoted sacrifice in which the martyrs gave their lives for the Church. These are hard times all round, and we may well meet harder times before long ; and we Catholics shall feel them not least, with the burden of large families and the burden of supporting our children's education. We shall grumble, sometimes, at the sacrifices demanded of us. But before we grumble, let us pause awhile on the old bridge and think of three men, Nicholas Garlick, Robert Ludham, and Richard Simpson, who were butchered there in cold blood, when times were worse than ours. God grant, through the prayers of all the English martyrs, that we ourselves may not be found wanting in whatever trials his mercy may suffer us to undergo.

XIX. BERNADETTE OF LOURDES

Put off the shoes from thy feet, for the place whereon thou standest is holy ground. *Exodus* iii, 5.

ABOUT three thousand years ago, a man stood, thrilled with religious awe, on the slopes of Mount Sinai in Arabia. He was a shepherd, feeding on those barren pastures the flocks of his father-in-law ; his attention had been aroused, at a distance,

by the unwonted sight of a fire in the desert scrub.
And now that he had drawn nearer, he saw that this
was not merely something beyond the ordinary, but
something beyond nature itself; the bush before
which he stood burned continually, but was not consumed. At the same time a divine warning came to
him that he must take off the shoes from his feet in
sign of reverence. He did so, and when he had done
so the Divine Voice came to him again; he was to
bear a message to his brethren, the children of Israel,
subject at that time to a barbarous captivity in Egypt.
The God of their fathers, the God of Abraham and
Isaac and Jacob, would deliver them from that
bondage; and when they had come out of Egypt,
they were to do sacrifice to him on this mountain of
Sinai. And, in token of the new covenant he was to
make with his people, the God of Abraham and Isaac
and Jacob revealed himself by a new name: I AM
WHO AM.

Rather less than eighty years ago, a little girl stood
before the rock of Massabieille, in the township of
Lourdes, on the slopes of the Pyrenees. No premonition of any divine event disturbed her thoughts; she
was at play with her companions, and if she took off
the shoes from her feet it was only to cross the stream
that lay in their path. She heard a noise, like that of a
strong wind; she turned, and saw that the trees in
the valley were not bowed as a strong wind must bow
them. She turned back towards the rock, and a rose-
bush that grew in front of it. And now she saw the
rose-bush flaming with something more bright, more
pure, more beautiful than fire. She saw above it the
figure of a Lady; what need to describe it in detail?
Wherever Christendom reaches, the helpless aspirations
of Christian artists have made that figure familiar to
every human eye. The Lady said no word, but she

made one sign, the Sign of the Cross ; and the little girl, taking courage, said her rosary as if to defend her from harm. Then the Vision beckoned to her to come nearer ; she drew back in alarm, and it vanished. She took off her other stocking, crossed the stream, and rejoined her companions, who had seen nothing. That was all ; it was only in later visits that she realized what a grace had been bestowed upon her ; that she, too, was to lead a world out of its captivity ; draw it after her to worship God and celebrate the glories of his Mother on that mountain. It was only many days later that the gracious Lady revealed herself by name ; lifted up her eyes to heaven and said : ' I am the Immaculate Conception.'

Moses was a shepherd, not by choice. A man of courts and palaces, he had been driven into exile, and served, in that exile, his apprenticeship among the flocks. It is curious how often God has chosen a shepherd when he has wanted to impart an inspiration that has revolutionized men's lives. Jacob was a shepherd, the founder of the Jewish race ; David was a shepherd, the ancestor of its royal dynasty ; Amos was a shepherd, the first of its sons to prophesy and to commit his prophecies to writing. And under the new dispensation it is not otherwise ; the shepherds at Bethlehem were the first to hear from their cronies, the Angels, of the Divine-Human Birth, and you will find shepherd Saints in every age of Christian piety— St. Geneviève, St. Paschal Baylon, St. Vincent de Paul, St. John Vianney. Curious, did we say ? There is nothing curious about it when you come to think of it. For God himself was content to be described by his ancient people as a Shepherd ; ' Hear, thou shepherd of Israel,' ' The Lord is my shepherd,' ' He shall feed his flock like a shepherd ' ; and when the Divine Word came to dwell among us, he chose for

himself the title of the Good Shepherd, and handed it
on to St. Peter, his favourite Apostle, when he committed to him the care of all the churches. He who
would lead God's people must imitate the Divine fore-
thought, the Divine patience, the Divine gentleness
which tends and pursues so lovingly the straying hearts
of men. Shepherd to shepherd, God delegates to
Moses his pastoral office.

St. Bernadette, too, was a shepherd girl. Not that
this was her business in her father's home ; but when
she went on a visit to friends of the family at Bartres,
the year before her apparitions, she was given charge
of a flock of sheep, among which, characteristically,
she made the tiniest lamb her favourite. So she, too,
was apprenticed to the shepherd's trade ; for she, too,
was to be the leader of God's people. And the gracious
Lady who appeared to her over the rose-bush, was not
she the daughter of a shepherd, St. Joachim ? And
will not she, like Rachel before her, have fed her
father's flock ? Shepherdess to shepherdess, our
Lady delegates to St. Bernadette her pastoral office.

Moses led his people, and they followed him, where ?
To the same mountain in which he had first been
privileged with the intimacy of Almighty God. We
were picturing, just now, a solitary figure in the
desert, alone with God, no other human creature in
sight. Carry your mind forward a little space of time,
and you will see the same man closeted once more
with the same Divine Audience ; but, at the foot of
the mountain, what is this ? A vast array of Bedouin
tents, the migration of a people. More than six hundred thousand souls worshipping God in the mountain
he had chosen. With all that, the vision is still for
Moses, and for Moses only. The people stand at the
foot of the mountain, with limits appointed to them
which they must not transgress ; Moses goes up into

the mountain, and is hidden by a dark cloud from
mortal view.   The people see the play of lightning
round the summit, but the Divine Voice is not for
them ; it is only through Moses that the word comes
to them.   Yet that word is sovereign ; centuries go by,
and the nation of Israel increases as the sand by the
seashore, but still the memory of Sinai haunts them,
and their dearest traditions are all prefaced with the
same rubric, ' Moses said.'

Bernadette stood before the grotto on the eleventh
of February with no other human creature near her,
except two little girls, her companions, on the other
side of the stream.   When she knelt there on the fourth
of March, just three weeks later, she was being
watched by a crowd of twenty thousand pilgrims.   Yet
still the vision was only for her ; for those others there
was nothing but the grotto and the rose-bush, and the
mountains beyond.   They could see the smile that lit
up the face of the visionary, but that was all.   But the
memory of her smile still haunts the grotto, and all
Christendom flocks there in its hundreds of thousands,
to worship in the place where her feet stood.   And still
she haunts the place like a visible presence ; when
you offer your lighted candle, you half expect to hear
her cry out : ' You're burning me ! ' as she did when
she woke from her ecstasy nearly eighty years ago.

When Moses came down from the mountain, his
face shone, so that the children of Israel could not
bear to look upon it.   They saw there, as if reflected
in a frail human mirror, the glory of him who had
spoken with him on the mount.   And Moses covered
his face with a veil, lest even that reflected radiance
should be profaned by human sight.

In May, 1866, the chapel which Bernadette's ecstasies
had demanded was inaugurated at Lourdes.   That
July she took the veil with the Sisters of Charity of

Nevers, and Lourdes was not to see her again. Did we think that she would wait there to tell us all her story, to touch our rosaries and sign our autograph books ? No, the face which had looked into the face of the Immaculate must be veiled thenceforward ; thenceforward we should not even see her smile.

Moses was sent to deliver his people from bondage, and from a bondage to which they had grown accustomed, so that they loved their fetters, and were constantly turning on him and asking why he could not leave them alone. That was his chief difficulty— they did not want to be set free. And even when they had been set free, and led out into the wilderness, they were always hankering after the luxuries they had enjoyed in Egypt, always murmuring against the rough fare of the desert. While Moses was up in the mountain, the people he had left behind him in the valley made a golden calf and fell to worshipping it, as they had worshipped it in Egypt. All his life he preached to an incredulous race, condemned, for their hardness of heart, to forty years' wandering in the wilderness before they achieved their promised resting-place.

Bernadette was sent to a world in bondage, and to a world which rejoiced in its bondage. Those apparitions of hers took place in the very middle of the Victorian age, when mankind, or at any rate, the richer part of mankind, was enjoying material plenty to a degree, I suppose, unexampled before or since. And the presence of material plenty had given rise to a general spirit of materialism ; a spirit which loves the good things of this life and is content with the good things of this life, does not know how to enlarge its horizons and think about eternity. She was sent to deliver us from that captivity of thought ; to make us forget the idols of our prosperity, and learn afresh the meaning of suffering and the thirst for God. That is what Lourdes is for ; that is what Lourdes is about— the miracles are only a by-product. You might have thought that in our day, when prosperity has waned and all of us, or nearly all of us, have to be content with less, we should have needed no longer these Divine warnings from the rock of Massabieille. We know that it is not so ; we know that in this wilderness of drifting uncertainties, our modern world, we still cling to the old standard of values, still celebrate, with what conviction we may, the worship of the Golden Calf. The year of Bernadette's canonization finds us no less in need of public reparation for our common sinfulness than the year in which Bernadette took the veil.

Do not think me fanciful, then, if I suggest that we ought to see in Lourdes a sort of modern Sinai ; and that we ought to treasure the words our Lady spoke in the grotto as we treasure the words God spoke to Moses on the mountain. Ten words of God to Moses, which are enshrined, now, in the general conscience of humanity ; ten words of our Lady to St. Bernadette, ruling principles (surely) for the Church to whose altars the little prophetess has been raised. Let us meditate them, very briefly, as they come.

At the third apparition, St. Bernadette took with her pen and ink and a sheet of paper, to write down the commands which, she felt, the strange Lady would want to express. And the first recorded utterance of the Immaculate bears on that point ; 'What I have to tell you, I do not need to set down in writing. Will you have the kindness to come here for a whole fort-night ? ' When Moses came down from Mount Sinai, he brought with him two tables of stone, on which the Ten Commandments had been written, we know not how, by Almighty God himself. But the Christian law, St. Paul tells us, is not written on tables of stone, but on fleshy tables of the heart. It is not a code of directions exterior to ourselves, but a spirit with which we are to be imbued, an attitude which we are to assimilate. And Bernadette, accordingly, must not expect her decalogue to be registered in pen and ink. She must come to the grotto for a fortnight, as continuously as she may, and the message will write itself on her heart. And from us, too, our Lady of Lourdes asks no laborious exercise of the intellect, no feats of memory, if we are to learn her lesson. We are to watch Bernadette, and see our Lady's own image in her.

That was the first word, and the second word followed immediately, with an almost cruel abruptness : ' I do not promise you that you will be happy in this world, but in the next.' Moses, the servant of God, brought his people out into a land flowing with milk and honey —but he was not allowed to enter that promised land himself. And St. Bernadette was to open for us that miraculous spring from which healing has flowed into thousands of homes ; the grotto in which she worshipped is hung about with a forest of crutches, the trophies of our Lady's clients ; but St. Bernadette herself, what reward was given to her for all her faith and endurance ? Thirteen short years of life in the cloister ; years haunted with the premonition, and crowned with the experience, of long and continued bodily suffering. We had so often been told, yet nothing really succeeded in making us believe, that it is eternity which matters, and time does not count. Bernadette should be a living proof of that doctrine ; our Lady's favourite confidante, rewarded, not with health like us others, but with a short life and a long cross !

At the fifth apparition, during forty minutes of ecstasy our Lady taught St. Bernadette, word by word, a special prayer she was to use. That prayer she learned by heart, and used it every day for the rest of her life.

What was it ? we ask, breathlessly. The answer is that we do not know, and shall never know till, by God's grace, we are allowed to use it in heaven. The message, I say it again, was for Bernadette, and for us only through her ; we are not to go to Lourdes for this or that ceremony, this or that form of prayer ; it is to be the shrine not of a ritual but of a life.

And the fourth word presses on to the heart of the mystery ; it was during the sixth apparition that our Lady said suddenly, ' Pray for sinners.' That is not what we think of, is it, when people ask us what are the most characteristic impressions we carried away from the Lourdes pilgrimage. We think of those wasted forms in their invalid chairs grouped round the square in the afternoon, and the heart-rending petitions that echo round them, Lord, grant that I may see, Lord, grant that I may hear, Lord, grant that I may walk. Or we think of the torchlight procession in the evening, and the singing of the Credo which concludes it ; we remember Lourdes as the embodiment of a great act of faith. But when our Lady stood at the grotto, the first command she gave was not, Heal the sick ; was not, Convert the unbeliever. Her command was, Pray for sinners. Man's sin, that is our real malady ; man's impenitence, that is the crying problem.

The fifth word is unique, in that it was heard by the bystanders, not indeed from our Lady's lips, but from Bernadette's. As she knelt there in ecstasy, she repeated several times, sobbing, the one word, ' Penance.' They learned afterwards that she was repeating it after our Lady. This, then, is our Lady's one public utterance ; and, as I say, it is the message of Lourdes. We are to make there, in common, what reparation we can for our common faults. The true music of Lourdes is not the ' Lord, he whom thou lovest is

sick ' that thunders across the square ; not the *Ave, Ave,*
that sweeps down the terraces.   It is the *Parce, Domine,*
parce populo tuo—the confession of our sins, and a
desperate cry for pardon.

Then, not till then, at the ninth apparition, our Lady
pointed to the sacred spring, and bade her prophetess
drink and wash there.   This sixth word is a kind of
interlude ; and, remember, our Lady never said that
those who drank, those who washed, would be healed
of their bodily infirmities.   The faithful themselves
were left to find out that gracious corollary ; the
ceremony performed at the time by St. Bernadette
was rather a pantomime of humiliation—to eat grass
like the cattle, to drink and wash in a muddy spring.
She dedicated herself and her mission to human
scorn.

The seventh word emphasises the lesson of humiliation, and connects it with the lesson of penance. ' You
will kiss the ground, for sinners.' Because all our worst
sins take their origin in pride, the penance we are to
offer—we moderns at least—must be prefaced by the
mortification of reminding ourselves, what and whence
we are. So, next Wednesday, we open our Lenten fast
by having our foreheads smeared with ashes, while the
priest says to us, as God said to Adam when he had
sinned : ' Dust thou art, and unto dust shalt thou
return.' We must learn to grovel before we can learn
to weep.

With the eighth and ninth words we come at last
to practical, rubrical directions, which will serve to
organize Bernadette's revelations as a cult. ' Go and
tell the priests to build me a chapel ' ; ' I want people
to come here in procession.' Man is made of body and
soul ; body as well as soul must take part in his self-
dedication to God. Material edifices, of wood and
stone, outward gestures, pilgrimage and march and

song, must be the complement and the expression of his inward attitude. So, when God issued to Moses his moral law, in all the grandeur of its austerity, he directed at the same time the building of a tabernacle, and the rites which were to be performed in and at the tabernacle ; he would enlist material things in the service of a spiritual ideal. So, when our Lady preached to Bernadette her gospel of penance, she externalized it and eternalized it by prescribing the outward ceremonies that should be its expression.

The tenth word is the best known of all : ' I am the Immaculate Conception.' Why (people have asked) did she say that, rather than ' I am the immaculately conceived?' It is, perhaps, rash to venture on explanations. But when God appeared to Moses, he revealed himself under the title I AM WHO AM ; and theologians have read in those simple words the most profound truth about the Divine Being—that there is no distinction of Essence and Existence, of Attributes and Personality, in him ; his Goodness, his Wisdom, his Power, his Justice, are nothing other than himself. That cannot be said, obviously, of any creature. But, may we not suppose that the plenitude of grace which flowed into the soul of our Blessed Lady so overshadowed and transformed her human personality as to make her little suppliant forgetful of it ; make her see, there in the grotto, no longer a human figure but the embodiment of a spiritual truth ? That the thought of what she was and is was obscured, in that moment of revelation, by the thought of what God wrought and works in her ?

' To-day, if you will hear his voice, harden not your hearts,' was the message of Sinai. Moses struck the hard rock, and the waters gushed out ; he could not wring tears, even so, from the hearts of a stubborn people. Surely, when she pointed to the miraculous spring at Lourdes, our Lady was telling a whole world to weep for its sins. So many years have passed, and do we still come away from Lourdes dry-eyed ?

XX. LISIEUX AND ASSISI

Except you shall be converted, and become as little children, you shall not enter into the kingdom of heaven. *Matthew* xviii, 3.

YESTERDAY, Christendom was celebrating one of the most recent, one of the most widely loved, among the memories of God's Saints ; the third of October commemorates St. Theresa of Lisieux, the Little Flower of Jesus. The prayer of the feast asks that we may follow her footsteps in humbleness and simplicity of heart. I am not absolutely certain, but I think that that is the only place in the whole of the Church's liturgy in which we pray God to make us simple. It is as if the Little Flower had discovered, for herself, a new Christian virtue. Of course, that is not really so. All the Saints have practised all the virtues, except for some of those who reached their crown through martyrdom. But it may sometimes happen that one particular virtue shines out in the life of one particular Saint more evidently than in the life of any other. The Saints, you see, are our Lord's crown ; and in that crown one particular jewel catches the light, now and again, so as to shine out more than ever. All the Saints have possessed the virtue of simplicity ; but it was not till God saw fit to give us a really glaring example of saintly simplicity in St. Theresa that the Church really noticed what a wonderful thing it is.

If we doubted that there was simplicity to be found

among the Saints, or even that there was a high degree of simplicity to be found among the Saints, before the Little Flower came, those doubts were not able to last after October the third. October the fourth has brought with it the memory of another Saint, once more one of the most dearly loved in Christendom, who also strikes the imagination by his simplicity perhaps more than by any other gift; I mean, of course, St. Francis. In a curious way, the Poor Man of Assisi and the young nun of Lisieux stretch out hands to one another across the centuries, as if they were two children playing a children's game together—Ring a ring of roses, perhaps. I do not think it is fanciful, in spite of the difference in their centuries and their careers, to mention these two Saints in the same breath. To take just one instance, and a not very important instance—you can see the same child-like quality in each of them if you consider their fondness for make-believe. The Little Flower, you remember, when she was encouraging her novices to pray for the conversion of sinners, told them to think of those souls as a set of nine-pins, and those prayers as a ball trying to knock down first one and then another. And she was always indulging in fantasies of that kind; so was St. Francis. When he felt tempted, one extremely cold night, to regret his vows, he got up out of bed, and went out into the snow just as he was, and made a snow woman and six snow children; and he pretended that they were his wife and family. 'There,' he said to himself—for he talked to himself, as all children do—'these must all be clothed; see, poor things, they are dying of cold; here there will be all kinds of trouble.' When you read stories like that, you realize that it is not a very long way from the Little Flowers of St. Francis to the Little Flower of Jesus.

But, of course, there was all the difference in the world between the opportunities these two had of shewing their child-like qualities to the world at large. St. Theresa says in her life, addressing her superior, who was also her sister : ' An artist must have at least two brushes ; the first, which is the more useful, gives the ground tints and rapidly covers the whole canvas ; the other, a smaller one, is employed for the details of the picture. You, my dear Mother, represent the valuable brush our Lord holds lovingly in his hand when he wishes to do some great work in the souls of his children, and I am the little one he deigns to use afterwards to fill in the minor details.' If you will put on one side the modesty of those expressions, they give you an admirable description of the difference between St. Theresa and St. Francis. St. Theresa is the little brush ; her work for God consists in etching in, very carefully, all the little daily details of a cloistered life with enormous care, like one of the pre-Raphaelite painters, drawing every leaf and every stone with minute precision. Whereas St. Francis is the impressionist ; he gets his effects with broad sweeps of the brush. He will fill the world with friars, men who have a roving commission to do nothing in particular except imitate Jesus Christ ; his ideas are big enough, even, to make him go off to the East and try to convert the Sultan to the Christian faith ; his vision cannot be bounded by continents—that is the difference.

Not that that was a difference of temperament ; rather a difference of circumstances. St. Theresa's career reminds you of those lines of Henry Vaughan :

If a star were confined into a tomb,
   Her captive flames must needs burn there ;
But when the hand that locked her up gives room,
   She'll shine through all the sphere.

God locked up St. Theresa in the tomb of a Carmelite convent ; he would shew a miracle of his power by making her suddenly shine through all the sphere only after she was given room, only after her bodily death. So she lived in her Carmel like a child that is shut indoors on a rainy day. She would have liked to be converting the heathen, shedding her blood as a martyr ; that was not for her, so she made the best of the little world she lived in, as a child will make the best of staying indoors when it becomes clear that the rain is not going to stop. By her power of make-believe—and what it made her believe was no more than the truth—she would turn her Carmel and the little opportunities of her life at Carmel into a glorious mission for winning the souls of men. But St. Francis was different—God never locked *him* into a tomb. Think of St. Francis as you will, you always think of him as in the open air. He was a schoolboy out for a holiday, you might almost say a schoolboy playing truant from school.

All St. Francis' life was a sort of holy picnic. There is one story of his sitting down to a meal, a very simple and we should think rather an unpleasant meal, beside a spring with rocks and trees round it ; and all through the meal he kept on exclaiming : ' What a treasure we have here, what a treasure ! ' Now, St. Francis was not one of your sophisticated modern people, who could get enthusiastic about the beauties of nature because he thought it was the proper thing to do. No, he really enjoyed the treat as a child enjoys its picnic ; it was so kind of God to have arranged a setting of rocks and trees for him like that. And that is the secret, of course, of his love of creatures. Do not by the way, ever let anybody try to make you believe that St. Francis was fond of animals ; he was fond of creatures. His brother was the sun, his sister the moon ; when he had to have an operation on his eyes, without anæsthetics, he asked his brother fire to be gentle to him, and when the last scene of all came, he could welcome his sister death. Anybody can be fond of live animals because they remind him of human beings ; grown-up people often are, and some of them are very sloppy about it. But it is the child that can manage to be fond of inanimate things, talk for hours to a stuffed bird, for example. And St. Francis was like that ; he loved creatures, not because they reminded him of human beings, but because they reminded him of God.

Now, what is this gift of simplicity, which we admire so much in children, because it is natural ; which we admire so much in the Saints, because it is super-natural ? Do let us get rid at once of a favourite mis-take ; that of supposing that to be simple means to be ignorant. You see, there is only one Being who is absolutely simple ; that is Almighty God, and he knows everything. No, to be simple is to see things with the eye of God, that is, to see them as they really are, without the trimmings. To be able to distinguish what is important for what is incidental and doesn't matter ; to get down to the broad, primary truths, and forget what is merely conventional. I think if you asked me who was the simplest person I have ever known I should mention the name of one of the cleverest men of our generation, Mr. G. K. Chesterton, who died this summer. And it is not out of place to mention him here, because he was perhaps the best biographer St. Francis ever had, and he died when he had just come back from a visit to Lisieux. I remem-ber he says somewhere that, if you find a man lying dead under the sofa, you explain the situation to other people by saying : There is a man lying dead under the sofa ; you don't say : There is a man of considerable refinement lying dead under the sofa. On such occasions you keep to the essential facts ; and that is what simplicity means, to keep to the essential facts ; not just at moments, but all your life.

And for the Saint, you see, the essential facts are those of the next world, rather than those of this. God, your soul, eternity, sin, judgement, those are the essential facts ; and the simplicity of the Saints is to distinguish those facts all the time, without effort, from the unessential facts that do not matter, although human vanity and snobbishness and worldliness think they do. How are we going to get that spirit ourselves ? I think it is easy to see how St. Francis got it ; what was the first stage, anyhow, in the getting of it. He cut himself off entirely from all worldly possessions. That is why I was telling you just now he soliloquized like that over the snow-woman, his imaginary wife. ' Here there will be all sorts of trouble,' he said to himself ; he reminded himself that his vow of chastity had saved him from a whole heap of anxieties which might have distorted that simplicity of vision with which he saw God. It was the same with his poverty. When his father summoned him before the bishop, and said he would have no more to do with him and would cut him off from his inheritance, he immediately took off his clothes, because they really belonged to his father, and went about in a piece of old sacking with a cross marked on it. Now, he said, he could really understand what it was to have a Father in heaven. I have called St. Francis a truant schoolboy, and that is what he was ; he ran away from the world and its belongings so as to keep holiday in his heart to God.

Well, we cannot do that ; our state of life and the demands which other people's lives make on our own will not allow us to do that. All right ; but, remember, the less we cling to worldly enjoyments, the more we accustom ourselves to do without worldly enjoyments, the better chance we shall have of cultivating that true simplicity which is the simplicity of the Saints. The world is very old nowadays, and we are all very grown-up ; you can buy the wisdom of the ages for a shilling on a bookstall ; the newspapers fling problems at us, and the advertisements tell us that it is our duty to get on, to make money, and to want as much as possible. That is what we call a high standard of living, to want as much as possible. Conventions of civilization, the second servant and the fresh suit on Sundays and the latest fashion in hats and in eye-brows make life expensive for us and complicated. But with all these wonderful opportunities, is our world really a happy world ? Can we look back at the age of St. Francis without feeling something of regret for our own childhood, something of that twinge which comes to us when we see, in the house where we were brought up, the familiar passage that leads to the nursery door ?

The more we can resist the tyranny of these worldly embarrassments, the more we can be content to live according to our income, to be wise according to our opportunities, to be ourselves, to laugh at shams and see things as they are, the more we shall imitate St. Francis, and the better compliment we shall pay him. May his prayers, and the prayers of our Blessed Lady and St. Theresa, bring us out of this world, our schoolroom, into the glorious liberty of the sons of God.

XXI. G. K. CHESTERTON

Blessed are they that saw thee and were honoured with thy friendship. For we live only in our life, but after death our name shall not be such. *Ecclesiasticus* xlviii, 11.

THE man whom we laid to rest the other day in the cemetery at Beaconsfield was one of the very greatest men of his time. If posterity neglects him, it will pronounce judgement not upon him, but upon itself. He will almost certainly be remembered as a great and solitary figure in literature, an artist in words and ideas with an astonishing fecundity of imaginative vision. He will almost certainly be remembered as a prophet in an age of false prophets. He warned us in spacious times that human liberties were threatened, and to-day human liberties are in debate. He warned us in times of prosperity against the perils of industrialism, and industrialism is labouring for breath. He warned us, when imperialism was a fashion, that nationalism was a force not easily destroyed ; to-day nationalism is the shadow over men's hearts.

Whether he was a great author, whether he was a true prophet, does not concern him now—he lies deaf to the world's praise and secure from its catastrophes— nor does it concern us here. We are met, as Christians, to say farewell in our own fashion to a fellow-Christian who has outstripped us in the race for eternity. The most important thing about Chesterton, he would have been the first to say it, the most distinctive quality in Chesterton was a quality which he shared with some three hundred million of his fellow-men. He was a Catholic. The public discovered him in the early

years of the century. It was not till twenty years later
that he discovered himself. There is a legend told of
his absent-mindedness that he once telegraphed home
the words, ' Am in Liverpool ; where ought I to be ? '
And it took him fourteen years after the publication of
his book *Orthodoxy* to find out that he ought to be in
Rome.

I hope I do not wrong such a man in preaching his
panegyric, when I confine myself to considering the
position which belongs to him as a religious force ;
what Catholicism meant to him, and what he meant
to Catholicism. In the case of a meaner man we should
be content to celebrate his domestic virtues, his incon-
spicuous acts of charity. But Chesterton moved,
though with the personal simplicity of a child, in a
world of apocalyptic images ; he saw his religion
everywhere ; it mattered furiously to him. What he
did is in God's hands ; what he was is a matter of
gracious recollection to his friends ; it is the effect he
made on the world that claims the world's attention and
its gratitude.

I would speak first of the influence which Chesterton's earlier works had, on young men for the most part
and on Protestants. And it is the only claim I have to
stand here, in the place of older and closer friends,
that at the time when his earlier works were published,
I was myself a young man and a Protestant. I think it
is true to say that the generation which grew up between
the turn of the century and the Great War had a
tendency all the time to react in favour of religious
orthodoxy. The triumph of evolutionary materialism
had seemed complete ; the faith of Englishmen was
laid out for burial, with the cynics, the pessimists, the
positivists driving the last nails in its coffin. There
was a reaction of which we should hear more if the
events which began with 1914 had not decimated it

and left its less characteristic specimens to represent it.
I do not wish to discount the influence of other religious
leaders, Anglicans like Scott Holland or Catholics like
Hugh Benson. But the spear-head of that reaction
was a man so plainly on the side of the angels that you
did not stop to inquire whether he were an Anglican
or a Catholic, G. K. Chesterton. The brilliance of his
work, the wideness of his appeal set the fashion in
favour of a religious attitude which the fashion of an
earlier age had derided. He was conscious, himself,
of the change of atmosphere when he wrote the
introduction to his book, *The Man Who Was Thursday*.
It is an extraordinary book, written as if the publisher
had commissioned him to write something rather like
the *Pilgrim's Progress* in the style of the *Pickwick Papers*.
And the poem which introduces it is a song not of
triumph but of release from tension in the middle of
a conflict.

' But we were young ; we lived to see God break their
    bitter charms—
God and the good Republic came riding back in arms ;
We have seen the city of Mansoul even as it rocked,
    relieved—
Blessed are they that have not seen, but, being blind,
    believed.'

The direct effect of that reaction in stemming the tide
of religious liberalism has been in great part obliterated
by the War. Its indirect effect, in producing conversions to the Catholic faith, made itself felt only during
the War, when the annual figure of conversions went
up from eight thousand to ten and from ten to twelve,
where it has remained ever since. Meanwhile the
prophet, who had acted as a signpost for us, remained
himself outside the Church, content to fight a lonely
battle for the philosophy he could see was right but

could not see was ours. What changed him then four years after the Armistice ? What was the new momentum which lent impetus to his thought, so that he no longer believed, being blind, but saw ? I never knew yet a convert who could give a precise answer to that question. To give a precise answer we should have to understand, as we shall never understand it here, the economy of God's grace. We can only say that if it were possible to deserve the grace of conversion, Chesterton had deserved it for years as no other man did ; and, if he had to wait so long for it, there is hope in that for many a waiting soul, perhaps for some waiting soul here, which still cannot see the end of its despairs.

Meanwhile what had happened was, to Chesterton himself, admirably clear. He had the artist's eye which could suddenly see in some quite familiar object a new value ; he had the poet's intuition which could suddenly detect, in the tritest of phrases, a wealth of new meanings and of possibilities. The most salient quality, I think, of his writing is this gift of illuminating the ordinary, of finding in something trivial a type of the eternal. In the first of his books which really made a name for him, *The Napoleon of Notting Hill*, the story opens at a moment when a Government clerk, walking behind two friends in town coats, suddenly sees the buttons on their coats as two eyes, the slit underneath as a nose line ; he has a vision of his two friends as two dragons walking backwards away from him. There is a law (he says in that connection) written in the darkest of the books of life, and it is this : If you look at a thing nine hundred and ninety-nine times, you are perfectly safe ; if you look at it the thousandth time, you are in frightful danger of seeing it for the first time. That was all that happened when Chesterton was converted. He had looked for the thousandth time at

the Catholic faith and for the first time he saw it.
Nothing in the Church was new to him, and yet
everything was new to him ; he was like the man in
his own story who had wandered round the world in
order to see, with fresh eyes, his own home. That it
was his home, neither friend nor foe had doubted ;
men did not even dare to whisper to him the old
pathetic lie that converts are unhappy. Whether his
work as a Catholic has been as influential as the work
which he did when he was only a defender of Catholics,
is a question hard to resolve. He was no longer the
latest fashion ; he had reached the age at which most
men have had their say ; his health had begun to
decline, and he was overworked, partly through our
fault. Nor, I think, will the world ever give a just
hearing to one who has labelled himself a Catholic.
But this I will say, that, if every other line he wrote
should disappear from circulation, Catholic posterity
would still owe him an imperishable debt of gratitude,
so long as a copy of *The Everlasting Man* enriched its
libraries. This I will say, that whenever I ask an
inquirer whether he has read any Catholic books
his answer regularly begins, ' I've read some Chesterton, of course.'

' We live only in our life and after death our name
shall not be such ' ; few men of our time could refuse
that epitaph to Gilbert Chesterton. Meanwhile
' blessed are they that saw him and were honoured by
his friendship ' ; they found in him a living example of
charity, of chivalry, of unbelievable humility which
will remain with them, perhaps, as a more effective
document of Catholic verity than any word even he
wrote. But the familiar voice, with its high chuckle
of amusement, will reach us no longer ; he, whose
belief in immortality was so publicly influential, can
give us no whisper of reassurance, now that he knows.

Only we know what we would say if he heard the suggestion that nothing remains of him beyond what was interred at Beaconsfield.

> ' The sages have a hundred maps to give ;
>   They trace their crawling cosmos like a tree ;
> They rattle reason 'out through many a sieve
>   That stores the sand and lets the gold go free.
> And all these things are less than dust to me
>   Because my name is Lazarus and I live.'

THE END

OUR GUIDING STAR

A SHORT LIFE OF
ST. TERESA OF LISIEUX

BY

FATHER VERNON JOHNSON

WITH AN INTRODUCTION BY THE
REVEREND EDWARD TOWERS
D.D., Ph.D.

' *Little Teresa, whom you in America call the
Little Flower, but whom I call my Guiding
Star.*'

Pius XI to Cardinal Dougherty,

May 17, 1925.

CONTENTS

INTRODUCTION

THIS short life of St. Teresa of Lisieux bears a title which tells us at once what we ought to look for in its pages. The Saint is here called *Our Guiding Star*, and what we are to learn of her is not merely that she is a Little Flower whose perfume charms us with its fragrance and that from heaven she scatters an abundant shower of roses upon those who invoke her aid in their needs, but chiefly that she is a teacher who will lead us to holiness of life if we follow her guidance. This is a truth which has not always been recognized by those who claim to be devoted to her. Millions have loved her for the charm which breathes from every page of her wonderful Autobiography ; countless numbers have experienced the power of her intercession with God and have learnt to turn to her for favours both spiritual and temporal ; not so many have set themselves to mould their lives on the pattern which she has put before us. Yet it is surely clear that God raised her up precisely that she might be a teacher, a Guiding Star, in a type of holiness which He has judged best suited to these modern days.

The manner in which a young, unknown nun

in a small town of France, who died of consumption at the early age of twenty-four, suddenly won the hearts of the Catholic world by an autobiographical sketch which she had written in a cheap exercise book for her sisters is scarcely less astonishing than the wonders which God soon worked in richest profusion through her intercession. Why did God bring about this extraordinary propagation of devotion to the Little Flower ? Why did He mark it by so many miracles ? He does not act without a purpose and we may well ask ourselves what His purpose was. The answer assuredly is that He acted in this wonderful way because He had raised up Teresa Martin, in religion Sister Teresa of the Child Jesus and the Holy Face, to deliver a special message to our modern world, and He wished this message to be guaranteed by unmistakable signs of its divine origin. Perhaps of no other saint in the whole history of the Church, apart from the inspired writers of the New Testament, can it be said with greater certainty that he, or she, had a message to give us from God.

The message which St. Teresa of Lisieux was raised up to deliver is the doctrine of the Little Way of Spiritual Childhood. There are still some people who fancy that the teaching of St. Teresa, or at least the popular form which devotion to her has taken, has too much sentimentality about it and is, therefore, an effeminate

perversion of true spirituality. The truth is that
the Little Way of Spiritual Childhood rests on
the teaching of Our Lord Himself, embodies in
a practical form most profound theological
truths and has received the emphatic approval
of the Church. Speaking during the Papal Mass
on the day of the canonization of our Saint
Pope Pius XI expressed the hope that all the
faithful would make themselves worthy to take
part in an abundant effusion of graces through
the intercession of ' Little Teresa,' and then he
used these memorable words : ' But we hope
still more that they will study her attentively,
with a view to imitating her, becoming themselves
children, for without this they cannot, according
to the word of Christ, enter into the Kingdom of
Heaven. If this way of Spiritual Childhood were
to be universally followed, who can fail to see
how easily that reformation of human society
would be realized, which we set ourselves to
accomplish at the beginning of our Pontificate ? '

It is perhaps the chief merit of this short life
that it shows us clearly what St. Teresa of Lisieux
understood by her Little Way. To sum up her
teaching in a few words, we are to abandon
ourselves to God with all the loving simplicity of
a child who leaves itself with a sense of utmost
security in the arms of a loving father. This
means the recognition of certain great truths :
that God is Our Father who loves us ; that we
are too weak to do anything of ourselves for our

eternal salvation ; that Our Father in heaven
will most certainly look after us if we abandon
ourselves to Him. Hence our attitude towards
God must be marked by love, humility, confidence, simplicity. Such is the essence of the
Little Way of Spiritual Childhood, and from it
there follows a special attitude towards suffering
and sacrifice. St. Teresa practised no severe
bodily mortifications, but she made her life one
long and loving offering of innumerable little
sacrifices. Every day brings its inevitable incon-
veniences and provides opportunities for patience,
forbearance, self-suppression. Here was the
material which the Saint used for making
countless acts of love of God. She offered all
these things to Him, as a child might come running to its parent with all sorts of things which it
had picked up. And if great suffering came—as
come it did, almost overwhelmingly—she took
this gladly as the choice of her loving Father who,
she knew, would give the strength to bear it.
The Little Way must needs take us under the
shadow of the Cross for, as our author reminds us,
He who said : ' Unless you be converted and
become as little children, you shall not enter into
the kingdom of heaven,' said also : ' If any
man will come after me let him deny himself, and
take up his cross daily, and follow me.' But for
the soul that has learnt the fundamental principle
of Spiritual Childhood the thought of what God
may send has no terrors. All will be accepted

simply, trustfully, even gladly. The recognition of God's hand, both in allowing suffering to come and in supporting us in the bearing of it, will make all the difference, and to St. Teresa who teaches this gracious lesson we can apply the words with which Francis Thompson greeted Our Lady :

> Thou gentleness that dost enmoss and drape
> The Cross's rigorous austerity.

All those who endeavour to follow the Little Way of Spiritual Childhood under the protection of Our Guiding Star can be sure that she will obtain wonderful graces for them. She whose ambition it was to spend her eternity in doing good will be their companion, helping, encouraging, instructing. ' St. Teresa helps me greatly,' declared Pope Pius XI in the midst of the incessant cares which weighed him down. ' I see her in a special way, I feel her presence. Sometimes in particular circumstances I ask her for special strength and help, and I obtain these always according to my desire and my need at the right moment.' So will it ever be with those who truly love her and realize that true devotion to her consists not in seeking favours from her but in imitating her ; not in pleasant admiration of the charm of her life but in humble effort to make their own lives beautiful as hers was beautiful ; not in sentiment, but in betterment.

At the end of his address at the canonization of

the Saint Pope Pius XI uttered these words :
' We adopt as our own the prayer of the new
St. Teresa with which she ends her invaluable
autobiography : " O, Jesus, I entreat Thee to let
Thy Divine eyes rest upon a vast number of
little souls. I entreat Thee to choose in this
world a legion of little victims of Thy love." '

It is obviously in this spirit that the present
book has been written : with God's blessing it
will do much to make St. Teresa a Guiding Star
in these days of universal war and moral up-
heaval, teaching her lesson of love, confidence
and hope, even under the shadow of the Cross.
Now, more than ever, we need her Little Way
and her protection.

E. TOWERS.

Ushaw College,
    Durham.

CHAPTER ONE

LITTLE TERESA

SOMEWHERE about the year 1855 two young people met crossing the Bridge of St. Leonard in Alençon, a little town in the north of France. The young man's name was Louis Martin. The girl was Zelie Guérin. Zelie Guérin had been praying that Almighty God would show her whom she was to marry, and she had also prayed that her future union might be blessed with many children, all of whom might be in some way consecrated to God's service. She tells us that she was at once attracted by Louis Martin's dignified and distinguished manner. She did not know him, but an inner voice which seemed to her to be the voice of God spoke to her soul saying : 'This is the person whom I have prepared for you.' This meeting was the beginning of a friendship which gradually ripened into love and they were married on July 13, 1858, in the church of Notre Dame at Alençon. They took a little house in the Rue St. Blaize and there they made their home. In this home little Teresa was born.

Louis Martin earned his living as a watchmaker

and jeweller. You can still see the little shop which he owned. Zelie Guérin was a lace-maker. Alençon is celebrated for its lace, and Zelie was very clever at this work. After her marriage she continued to work at it in her spare time and in this way helped to support the family.

Both Louis and Zelie came from very devout Catholic families, families who at the risk of their lives had often hidden priests during the French Revolution.

Their great desire was to have a son who should be a priest or a missionary. In this they were disappointed. They had nine children ; but four of them died when they were quite little, and two of these were boys. The rest were all girls.

Little Teresa was the baby in this big family of nine ; but when she was born only four of the older children were alive—Marie, Pauline, Léonie, and Céline. Of these Marie was Teresa's godmother, while Céline, who was next in age to Teresa, was the one with whom she used to play and to whom she told all her little secrets. Yet it was her second sister, Pauline, whom she loved most and thought most of. This was strange, because Pauline was away a great deal at school and Teresa did not see much of her. When her mother would say to her : ' What are you thinking of ? ' she would always answer : ' I am thinking of Pauline.' One day she heard them

say that Pauline would be a nun. Without
knowing what being a nun meant, little Teresa
said to herself : ' I will be a nun too.'

As she was the baby of the family, everybody
loved Teresa and made much of her. With love
all round her she became a very loving and affectionate child. When she was quite tiny her sisters
used to smile at the thousand little ways in
which she tried to show her love to them all.

Little Teresa not only loved her father and
mother and sisters, she loved everything. She
loved her toys and games, but even more than
these she loved flowers and butterflies and birds.
Her father had a little garden where she used
to play. From this garden she would stagger
back to the house laden with flowers, with which
she would adorn the statue of Our Lady. Her
favourites were always the simple wild flowers
—daisies, buttercups, poppies and marguerites.
When she was older she told how she used, when
little, to be taken for walks, and how she had
gazed with delight at the trees and the fields and
had loved the long valleys and the distant views.

Teresa adored her father and mother, but
especially her mother. She would follow her
mother through the house, wherever she went.
She would not leave her for a moment. From the
mother we learn that little Teresa, though so
loving, had very definite little faults. Her mother
tells us that Teresa was very clever, absolutely
honest, and had a heart of gold, but that at the

same time she was very determined and never did things by halves. One day her sister, Léonie, who had outgrown her dolls, brought to her two little sisters a basket filled with clothes, pretty pieces of material and other trifles upon which her doll was laid telling them to choose what they liked. Céline chose a little ball of braid. Teresa, after a moment's pause, put out her hand and said : ' I choose all,' and went off with the lot, basket and all. At times she could be very stubborn. In one of her letters her mother writes : ' When little Teresa has said No, nothing will make her change. One might leave her all day in the cellar without getting her to say Yes. She would sooner sleep there.' Noticing this and wondering how far she would go in it, her mother said to her one day : ' Teresa, if you will kiss the ground I will give you a halfpenny.' Little Teresa, being tiny, had not far to stoop, and a halfpenny seemed a fortune to her ; but her pride was up in arms and she would not do it. Holding herself erect she said : ' No, thank you, Mama, I would rather do without the halfpenny.'

The one thing that Teresa's mother desired for her was that she should grow up to be a saint ; and that she should learn to love God above everything else. The mother knew that, if Teresa was to do this, she must fight a big battle with these faults, that it would mean for her many sacrifices of her pride, self-will and stubbornness. To help her to make these sacrifices her mother gave her a chaplet of beads. Every time she or Céline made a sacrifice of their pride they were to move a bead across.

So Teresa learned from the very beginning that self-sacrifice, self-control in little things, is the only way we can learn to love God and be really holy.

When she was four and a half years old, a great sorrow came to little Teresa, whose life up till then had been all happiness and sunshine. The mother, whom she loved more than anybody else, who had taught her so tenderly about the love of God and Heaven, became very ill.

With the hope of being cured, she went to Lourdes with the three children, Marie, Pauline and Léonie. Together they prayed fervently at the Grotto of Our Lady. The mother was bathed in the baths. When she was in the baths the pain ceased, but as soon as she was outside the pain began as usual. For her children's sake she wished to be cured, but she made a complete surrender of herself to God to do with her what He wished.

On their return home she got steadily worse. At last she became so ill that they had to send for the priest to give her Holy Unction and the last Sacraments. This scene made a great impression on Teresa, as she knelt by her weeping father. Two days afterwards her mother died.

After the funeral the family returned home

together and the five children stood looking silently at each other in their grief. Seeing them like this, the maid exclaimed : ' Poor little children, you have no mother.' Whereupon little Teresa, flinging herself into Pauline's arms, said : ' Pauline will be my mother.' From that moment Pauline, taking the mother's place, became the one to whom Teresa turned for help in all her troubles.

This sorrow made a great change in little Teresa. Instead of being lively and talkative she became timid, shy and so sensitive that she would very easily burst into tears. It was not till ten years later, when she was fourteen, that she became her merry, joyful self again. It is easy to understand why Teresa was changed. She could never again think of her home on earth as her real home. The mother who had taught her about the love of God and about Heaven had left her and was now herself in Heaven. So, to little Teresa, Heaven was now her real home. Her home on earth was broken and she was now always thinking of that home in Heaven. So at the age of four and a half Teresa was beginning to learn the lesson that everybody has to learn—that life on Earth is a pilgrimage, a journey which cannot last, because we are all on the way to that home in Heaven where there will be no more parting or sorrow, where we shall all be happy in the Love of God.

Not far from Alençon there is a little country

town called Lisieux. Here M. Guérin, the
brother of Teresa's mother, lived with his wife
and their little children.

In order that his motherless children should be
looked after by Mme Guérin, M. Martin decided
to move to Lisieux. He bought a house on the
outskirts of the town called Les Buissonnets,
which in English means The Shrubbery. It
was a delightful little house, standing in a garden
with beautiful trees and flowers and surrounded
by a high French wall.

In the peace and quiet of this new home Pauline
watched over Teresa like a little mother. She
gave her her daily lessons and taught her to read
and write and, above all, taught her her cate-
chism and helped her to overcome her little
faults and so to grow in that love of God which
she had first learned from their mother. During
these days her father, seeing how she missed her
mother, was specially devoted to her. One of
her little games was to put seeds and bits of bark
into water to see what the mixture looked like.
If it turned out a pretty colour she used to put
it in a little cup and coax her father to drink it.
With a smile he would pretend to drink, while
taking very good care not to do so. In the garden
wall there was a little recess. Here she used to
make little altars and decorate them with flowers.
Then she would take her father by the hand to
the spot and insist on his admiring them, whatever they looked like. Sometimes he took her

for walks. On one of these walks he took her to pay a visit to the Blessed Sacrament in the Carmel Chapel. ' Look, little one,' he said, pointing to the grille, ' behind there are the holy nuns who are always praying.' So for the first time Teresa came in touch with Carmel. Nine years later, in that chapel, she took the veil.

Sometimes her father took her with him when he went fishing. While he fished she would sit in the field among the flowers. She still loved the field and flowers ; but now there was a difference. She was always thinking of her mother and, in her own words : ' I listened to the murmuring of the wind. Earth seemed a place of exile, I dreamed of Heaven.' On one of these occasions a violent thunderstorm came on. A thunderbolt fell in a field close by them. Teresa was not the least bit frightened ; but her father was. Several meadows separated them from the road. Though hampered with his fishing tackle, he took her up in his arms and carried her to safety, she all the time enjoying the lightning and the rain.

Teresa, with her long golden hair, her sweet smile and her clear, deep eyes, was growing a beautiful child. One day a lady, walking with her husband, remarked in a low tone as they passed : ' What a pretty little girl,' and asked M. Martin if she was his daughter. The father, though pleased, made a sign to them not to praise the child. But little Teresa noticed it and, she tells us, she couldn't help feeling a little bit pleased. But she had been far too well taught by her mother to be spoilt by flattery. Her mind was full of something else, and that was the love of the God Who had taken her mother to be with Him in Heaven. 'As I grew up,' she says, ' I loved God more and more and I frequently made Him the offering of my heart, using the words my mother had taught me. I strove to please Jesus in all my actions and I guarded with great care against ever offending Him.'

Thus the first three years of little Teresa's life after her mother's death were spent in the loving atmosphere of Les Buissonnets. But when she was eight years old her father decided to send her to school at the Benedictine Abbey at Lisieux. Teresa was so exceptionally quick that she was placed in a class with girls much older than herself, one or two being as much as fourteen years old. In spite of this she soon found herself at the top of the class. This made the other girls very jealous. Another thing which annoyed them was the fact that the nuns could not help noticing how devout Teresa was at her cate-chism and her prayers. At the same time she found it difficult to enter into the games which the others enjoyed. In fact she was not good at school games. All this made her school life very difficult and increased her shyness. One little girl, who was specially jealous, did all she could to be unkind to little Teresa, made fun of her and turned the other girls against her. Teresa, being timid, did not know how to defend herself and used to go away and cry.

She had, however, the pleasure of showing her father, who often came to fetch her from school, the prizes she won in class. Moreover, the unkindness of the other girls did not destroy her own natural friendliness. Nor did their jealousy make them, as a whole, dislike her. She had a great gift for telling stories to which even the biggest girls liked to listen. In fact the mistresses had to stop the little orator, because they found the girls sat listening to her in playtime instead of getting the exercise which their games were meant to give them. This gift of inventiveness also came out in the games she made up to be played with her cousin, Marie Guérin. One of these games was pretending that they were hermits. They had a little hut in the garden and a small patch of vegetables. One of them would work while the other prayed. All went well until one day when they decided to imitate the modesty of hermits in the street. 'Lead me,' said Teresa to Marie, 'I am going to shut my eyes.' 'So am I,' said Marie. They thought they could safely do this so long as they stayed on the footpath. But unfortunately they fell over a box of oranges which had been left outside a shop door. Out ran the angry shopkeeper while the would-be hermits scrambled to their feet and made off at full speed, their eyes wide open and their recollection broken by the angry voice of her cousin, Jeanne Guérin, who was in charge of them.

Teresa had two other special friends among the girls at school. At one time one of these girls had to be absent from school for several months. Teresa thought very often about her while she was away, and when she came back she ran up to show her how glad she was to see her again. But the girl took practically no notice of her. Little Teresa's friendship was no longer wanted. Teresa felt this very keenly but said nothing. She never forgot her little friend and years afterwards she said : ' But I still love that little schoolfriend and continue to pray for her ; for God has given me a faithful heart and when once I love I love for ever.' Here already we have a glimpse of that unshakable loyalty which she showed all her life long, in spite of every obstacle, to her human friends and, above all, to Almighty God.

After Teresa had been at school about a year, Pauline, her beloved ' little mother,' told her that she was going to enter Carmel. Teresa was still suffering from the loss of her first mother. She was now to lose her second little mother. This was more than she could bear. Pauline was going away for ever. There would be no more happy evenings at Les Buissonnets. Teresa had never spoken of her school troubles at home because she did not like to complain. But, during the day, she had always had these evenings to look forward to. Now there would be no more of them. Her first visit to Pauline at Carmel only made it worse. For she was only allowed to see her little mother alone for two or three minutes, and then she could only see her behind a grating instead of sitting on her knee. She tells us later : ' I, who had been accustomed to talk to my little mother of all that was in my heart, could now scarcely snatch two or three minutes at the end of the family visit. I went away with my heart torn with grief. I kept saying " Pauline is lost to me." '

Ever since her mother's death Teresa had never been really well. This second shock was too much for her and she rapidly grew very ill. The doctors did all they could, but she only grew worse until at last the doctors and her family thought she was bound to die. Her father went to Paris to have a novena of Masses said for the cure of his little daughter at Notre Dame des Victoires.

On the Sunday evening during the novena Teresa became much worse and could not recognize any of her sisters. Marie went out to the garden. Léonie carried little Teresa to the window and pointed to Marie, who looked up and called : ' Teresa, my little Teresa.' It was no good ; Teresa did not seem even to see her. Léonie carried her back to bed and the three sisters, fearing lest she was about to die, for, humanly speaking, it seemed inevitable, fell on their knees before the statue of Our Lady which stood beside her bed. Marie implored Our Lady's assistance with all the fervour of a mother who begs the life of her child and will not be refused. Léonie and Céline joined in her prayer, and that cry of faith forced the gates of Heaven. Then Teresa, too, looked towards the statue. Let her tell the story in her own words : ' All at once the statue became alive. Our Lady became so beautiful that I shall never be able to describe her heavenly loveliness. Her face was so sweet, so good, so loving. But what touched me most was her wonderful smile. Then all my pain vanished. I began to cry silently, but my tears were tears of heavenly joy. She smiled at me. Then I lowered my eyes and in a moment I recognized all my sisters.' Teresa was completely cured.

To make sure that she should be quite strong before going back to school her father took her for a little holiday in the country. They went to stay with some friends who had a lovely castle in a beautiful garden. Teresa was given everything she wanted and, because she had been so terribly ill, everyone petted and spoiled her, flattering her and admiring her prettiness.

Little Teresa admits that she felt the charm of all this and how nice it was to be petted and spoiled. Yet something saved her from being really harmed by it all. That was the training which her mother had given her before she

died, which Pauline had so faithfully continued,
and which had taught her that the most important
thing in life is to love God, and that in order to
do that one must not be always thinking of one-
self, because if we do we shall love ourselves
more than we love Our Blessed Lord. Teresa
wrote some years afterwards : ' Perhaps Our
Lord wished me to know something of the world,
so that I might choose more deliberately the
way in which I had to follow Him.'

CHAPTER TWO

THE COMING OF THE VOCATION

FOUR years before her illness little Teresa had made her first Confession, in the old Cathedral of St. Pierre. It was a great event for her, and Pauline prepared her for it very carefully. 'Teresa, darling,' she said, 'it is not to a man but to God Himself that you are going to tell your sins.' This made a great impression on her little mind and, when they came to the Cathedral she asked Pauline : 'Shall I tell Father Ducellier that I love him with all my heart ? ' 'No, of course you can't,' said Pauline. 'Why do you want to ? ' She said : 'Well, isn't it God I am going to speak to ? ' When she reached the confessional she knelt down, but she was so tiny that the priest did not know she was there, so she had to stand up. The priest urged her to grow daily in devotion to Our Lady, and St. Teresa tells us : ' I determined to redouble my love for her who already filled so large a place in my heart.' After Confession was over she gave him her rosary to bless. When she got out to the street she stopped under a street lamp and took her newly blest rosary out of her pocket, turning it over and over. 'What are you looking at, Teresa, dear?' asked Pauline. To her amusement the reply she got was : 'I am looking to see what a blest rosary looks like.'

Now came the most important day that had ever dawned for her, the day of her First Communion. We have seen how, when she was very little, Mme Martin used to tell her about the love of Jesus for her soul. 'Teresa,' she would say, 'Jesus loves you and He made you to love Him. If you want to do this you must learn to do things to please Him even when they are hard to do and when you don't like doing them. One day you will see Him in Heaven ; meanwhile you must love Him on earth by little sacrifices. Jesus wants you to show your love to Him by giving yourself to Him as He has given Himself to you.'

So little Teresa was well prepared to understand the Love of Jesus in the Holy Mass, in which He gives Himself to us through sacrifice so that we, through sacrifice, may give ourselves to Him. From when she was quite a tiny child she had a great love for the Mass. One day she slipped out of the front door and started off in pouring rain though she had been told it was too wet for her to go to Mass. One Christmas Eve she begged Marie and Pauline to let her creep up between them to the Altar at the Midnight Mass, saying : 'I am so small nobody will see me.' One day when she was out for a walk she saw the Bishop on the other side of the street, and it was all her sisters could do to stop her running across the road to ask him if he would allow her to make her First Communion without waiting so long as she had been told she must do.

Now she was eleven, and the great day was coming near. Marie prepared her for it very carefully and, when she went down to Carmel to see Pauline, she, too, told her of the Love of Jesus for her in the Blessed Sacrament; and, just as her mother had given her the beads to encourage her to make her little acts of love, now Pauline gave her a charming little book to note down her acts of love and sacrifice. Every page in the book had a picture of a different kind of flower. This meant that every act she had to write down there was a little flower which she gave to Him to show her love. Before the First Communion she and some of the other little girls had a retreat at the Benedictine Convent. During the days of the retreat a nun used to come to little Teresa's bed at night, carrying a little lamp, and kiss her on the forehead. This nun showed Teresa such kindness that one night she said to her : 'Mother, I love you so much that I am going to tell you a secret.' Then she took the little book from under her pillow and showed it to the nun, her eyes sparkling with joy. At the end of the retreat she made three resolutions : (1) 'I will never give way to discouragement.'

(2) 'I will try to humble my pride.' (3) 'I will say the Memorare every day.'

At last the moment came for Teresa to kneel at the Altar and receive the sacred Host. Hear her own words : ' How sweet was the first embrace of Jesus ; it was indeed an embrace of love. I felt that I was loved, and I said : " I love Thee and I give Thee myself for ever." '

Here at the Altar in her First Communion we see the result of all that she had learned from her mother as a tiny little child and later on from Pauline in her catechism ; that is, that if you love anybody you want to forget yourself and do what pleases him, and that sacrifice becomes easy because you wish to put yourself out for those whom you really love. So, in her First Communion, she doesn't say just : ' I love You, Jesus,' but she adds these words, ' I give You myself for ever.' For Teresa love and sacrifice always went hand in hand. Jesus had loved her by giving Himself entirely for her ; she will now show her love to Him by giving herself entirely to Him. We shall see how this becomes the greatest wish of her life.

The happy day ended with a visit to Pauline at the Convent. There she saw her dear Pauline wearing, as she herself was, a white veil and a crown of roses, for Pauline had been professed, as Sister Agnes, that very day. This time there were no tears when Teresa had to leave ; for a long time now she had been feeling in her little heart that it was only in Carmel that she, too, would be able to give herself entirely to Jesus, as with all her heart she longed to do.

It was impossible for Teresa to love Our Lord and not to love other people. She knew that He Who had come to her soul at her First Communion did not come to her alone, but came also to others. Had she not knelt with her little schoolmates Jesus would have come for them, too, and not only for them, but for everybody in the world. Teresa realized this when she was quite a tiny. Her little heart went out to everybody, especially those who were poor or suffering.

When she was only six years old she met a poor cripple in the street. Thinking he wanted money, she offered him a penny. With a smile he refused it. Little Teresa was very distressed because she thought she had hurt him. Just at that moment her father had bought her a cake. Teresa wanted to run after the old man and give it to him, thinking to herself that, though he did not want money, he would like a cake, but she had not the courage to do so. There and then she said to herself : ' I will pray for my poor old man on the day of my First Communion.'

Five years later she faithfully kept her resolve.

In the spring of 1887 a horrible murder was committed in Paris by a man called Pranzini. The cruel murderer showed no sign of repentance, refused to see a priest or to have anything to do' with God. Little Teresa heard about this and she could not get him out of her mind. So she began to pray for him with all her soul and begged God to give her a sign that her prayer was answered, saying : ' This is my first sinner ; for that reason I beg You to give me a sign that he has repented.' Each day she eagerly looked at the papers for news. On September 1 she saw the story of his death. Struggling with his executioners, refusing to listen to the priest, he was dragged to the scaffold. Then, all of a sudden, at the very last moment, he turned round, asked for the chaplain's crucifix and kissed it three times. On reading this little Teresa had to run out of the room to hide her tears : she had been given her sign : the soul for whom she had prayed had been saved. What a sweet reply to her prayer.

Later in the year she went on pilgrimage to Rome, and a fellow-pilgrim handed her a magazine with stories of some missionary nuns. She took it eagerly, but then handed it to her sister, saying : ' I don't think I will read them, though I am longing to work for the salvation of souls. But God is calling me to be hidden in a cloister so as to give myself more completely to Him.' She told Céline secretly that the reason for this was in order that she might suffer more and by this means save more souls for Jesus, and specially to help priests in winning souls for Jesus.

Little Teresa prepared herself with very special

care and earnestness to receive the Sacrament of
Confirmation. The dignity of this Sacrament
and the graces which it bestows upon the soul
were more real to little Teresa than they usually
are to children. She received the Sacrament of
Confirmation on June 14, 1884. She tells us
herself : ' It was with the greatest care that I
made ready for the coming of the Holy Ghost
and I could not understand how anyone could do
otherwise before receiving this Sacrament of
Love. For some reason the ceremony was
delayed, so I had the consolation of having my
retreat prolonged. How happy I felt ! Like the
Apostles, I looked with joy for the promised
Comforter, gladdened by the thought that I
should soon be a perfect Christian, and have the
Holy Cross, the Symbol of that wonderful
Sacrament, traced upon my forehead for all
eternity. On that day I did not feel the mighty
wind of the first Pentecost, but I received the
gift of fortitude in suffering—a gift I needed
sorely for the martyrdom of my soul was soon
to begin.'

Speaking about little Teresa's Confirmation her
sister Céline says : ' The days immediately before
it are in particular deeply graven in my memory.
Thérèse, usually so calm, was no longer the
same ; a sort of enthusiasm and holy rapture
were visible in her manner. One day, during her
retreat, I expressed my astonishment at seeing
her thus. She then explained to me what she

understood regarding the power of this Sacrament and of the Holy Spirit taking possession of her whole being. There was in her words such conviction, in her countenance such ardour that, overcome by a sense of the supernatural, I came away deeply moved. The incident so struck me that I can see even now her actions, her attitude, the place where she stood and the memory of it will always remain.' Thus was little Teresa strengthened by her Confirmation with the gift of fortitude which she was soon to need so greatly and which was going to be such a mark of her spiritual life in the days that were to come.

Although little Teresa had been completely restored to health by Our Lady's smile, yet she had never recovered from that extreme sensitiveness from which she had suffered ever since her mother's death. At the time of her mother's death Teresa was four and a half years old, from that time her naturally happy disposition had deserted her, she became timid and shy and became so sensitive that a look was often sufficient to make her burst into tears. She could not bear to meet strangers, and was only really at ease at home in her own family circle. If she unintentionally offended anyone, instead of making the best of it she fretted until she became quite ill, thus increasing her fault instead of repairing it. Then she would cry at having cried : ' In fact,' she tells us, ' I made troubles out of everything, my extreme sensitiveness made me almost unbearable and all arguments against it were simply useless : I could not correct myself of this miserable failing. How then could I dare hope to be soon admitted into Carmel since nothing short of a miracle was required if my childish ways were to be altered.' But God wrought that miracle on December 25, 1886.

We will let her tell her story in her own words.

' On that blessed Christmas night, the sweet Infant Jesus, scarce yet an hour old, flooded with His glorious sunshine the darkness into which my soul was plunged. In becoming weak and little for love of me, He made me strong and brave, He placed His own weapons in my hands and I went from victory to victory. The fountain of my tears was dried up and from that time they flowed neither easily nor often. I must tell you here, dear Mother, the circumstances under which I received the priceless grace of my complete conversion. On reaching home, after Midnight Mass, I knew I should find my shoes in the chimney corner, filled with presents just as when I was a little child, a fact which proves that I was still treated as a baby. Papa loved to watch my enjoyment, and to hear my cries of delight as I drew each fresh surprise from the magic shoes, and his pleasure added considerably to mine.

' But the hour had come when Our Lord desired to free me from the failings of my childhood. He permitted that Papa, instead of indulging me in his usual way, should feel annoyed, and as I went upstairs I overheard him say : " All this is far too babyish for a big girl like Thérèse, and I hope this is the last time it will happen." These words cut me to the very heart and Céline, knowing how sensitive I was, whispered : " Don't go down just yet, you would only cry if you looked at your presents before Papa." ' But Thérèse was no longer the same—Jesus had transformed her. ' Choking back my tears, I ran down to the dining-room and making every effort to still the throbbing of my heart, I picked up my shoes and gaily drew out the presents one by one, looking all the time as happy as a queen. Papa joined in the laughter and there no longer appeared on his face the least sign of vexation.' Céline thought she must be dreaming, but happily it was a sweet reality and Thérèse had once for all regained the strength of mind which had left her when she was four and a half.

' On this radiant night began the third period of my life, the most beautiful of all, the most filled with heavenly favours. Satisfied with my good will Our Lord accomplished in an instant the work I had not been able to do during years. Love and a spirit of self-forgetfulness took complete possession of my heart, and thenceforward I was perfectly happy.'

From this moment little Teresa moves calmly and securely along the path of her vocation, undeterred by difficulties and never losing her inner peace in the midst of her greatest trial.

When Teresa was nearly fourteen, Marie, who had been looking after her during the last few years, thought she could now get on without her care ; therefore Marie felt herself free to enter Carmel, which she had for long wished to do.

Teresa had now left school and was having lessons from a lady who lived in Lisieux. This lady had many friends, and Teresa's father was anxious that his little girl should come in closer touch with the world. In this lady's house Teresa sat at a desk in an old-fashioned room where every day numbers of ladies came to see the lady of the house. Some of the visitors remarked on the new pupil's beautiful hair. Others asked in a whisper : ' Who is this pretty little girl ? ' Teresa, while supposed to be studying, heard and understood it all. ' These remarks,' she told her sister, ' pleased me very much, all the more as I knew those people meant what they said, because they did not know I could hear them.'

Fortunately this could do no harm to Teresa ; her heart was somewhere else ; she was longing more and more to enter Carmel. She felt she must do something about it, but what could she do? She was still only fourteen and a half. The Mother Prioress and Marie both thought she was too young to enter. ' I found only one person,' she said, ' to encourage me in my desire, my dear Pauline.' She must do something. Her courage was wonderful. She knew that the hardest thing to do was to tell her father, who was sixty-four and delicate. She knew she was his favourite and she felt she could not bear to leave him ; still she knew she must tell him. She chose the day of Pentecost and prayed the Holy Spirit to give her courage. It was a lovely summer evening and her father was sitting in the garden. Quietly, with her eyes filled with tears, Teresa slipped up to him and sat down beside him. ' What is it, my little Queen, tell me,' he said, drawing her close to him. Seeing she was in trouble he got up, put his arm round her and walked with her up and down the garden path. At last through her tears Teresa stammered out : ' I want to enter Carmel.' For a moment her father could not speak. Then he asked her to tell him why she wanted to do this. Teresa, feeling her confidence growing, was able to tell him quite simply. On the garden wall there grew a little plant with tiny white flowers. Her father stopped, loosened the little plant, roots and all, and gave it to her. It was a perfect little picture of what was happening to her. She had been brought up by her father in the garden home of Les Buissonnets : he was now giving her permission to be transplanted to the garden of Our Lady of Carmel. Teresa fastened her little white flower to a picture of Our Lady of Victories.

She preserved it carefully during all her life in Carmel, and kept it close to her in her last illness. The stalk, however, by that time had broken off close to the root. ' No doubt God wishes me,' she writes, ' to understand by this that He will soon sever all the earthly ties of His Little Flower, and will not leave her to fade here below.'

Little did her father know that, in giving her that little flower, he was giving her the name by which she should be known and loved throughout the world. Teresa had won her first victory.

But now she had something even more difficult to do. She had to win the consent of the Bishop. The very thought of it terrified her. She knew that her being so young would make a great difficulty. So, in order not to look any younger than she could help, she put up her hair for the first time. She had never visited anyone without her sisters before, now she had to begin with the Bishop. Her father went with her to the house, where they were received by the Bishop's secretary. Seeing tears in her eyes, he said : ' Ah, I see diamonds, you must not show those to the Bishop.' He took her into a big room where there were three large arm-chairs in front of a bright fire. Teresa was told to sit in the middle one. She tells us she found herself ' buried in an enormous chair where four little girls like me could have sat quite comfortably, far more comfortably than I did, for I was feeling terribly

frightened.' She told the Bishop all that was in
her heart and asked him to help her. The Bishop
asked her her reasons and she told him quite
simply. He listened kindly and, after talking a
little while with her, he said he must delay his
answer and that, in the meantime, he must have
a talk with Canon Delatroëtte, the Superior of
the Carmel. Teresa felt that nothing could be
worse, for Canon Delatroëtte had already refused
to let her enter. Tears came to her eyes. ' I
did more than show my diamonds to the Bishop,
I gave them to him, shedding tears.' The Bishop
felt very sorry for her and spoke very tenderly
to her. Then he took her round the garden to
show her the flowers and then said good-bye.
The visit was over ; Teresa had failed.

For the moment Teresa had failed, but she
did not give up hope. And now we are going to
see her showing all that same determination
which she showed as a little child.

Her father had arranged to take Céline and
Teresa on a pilgrimage to Rome. This gave her
one more chance. If only she could get the Pope
on her side. To do this she would have to speak
to him. Dare she ? She made up her mind to
have a try.

The day they started their pilgrimage they
spent a few hours in Paris. There they visited
the church of Our Lady of Victories and little
Teresa knelt at the shrine where the novena of
Masses had been offered to Our Lady for her

when she was so ill. There Teresa thanked the
Mother who had smiled on her for her wonderful
cure, and she asked her to keep her always safe
and to help her to obtain the great desire of her
heart.

Then they travelled through Switzerland.
Teresa had never seen anything like it : the
mountains with their precipices, the chalets,
the graceful belfries, the great lakes shining in
the sunset thrilled her. Teresa loved all this ; to
be cut off from it all would be a great wrench.
How could she make this sacrifice ? It was
because all this beauty, all this loveliness, spoke
to her of Him from Whom it all came, led her to
Him to Whom she wanted to give her life in
Carmel. She says : ' Later on, when I am in
Carmel and things are difficult I shall be able
to see only a little corner of the sky ; but I will
remember this scene, and the thought of it will
give me courage. I will not think of my own little
interests, but of the greatness of the power of
God. I will love Him alone and will not let
myself be troubled by little things, now that the
beauty of this world has given me a glimpse of the
loveliness of Heaven.'

When they arrived in Italy the first town they
visited was Milan. There they went to see the
Cathedral of wonderful white marble. To climb
to the top of the Cathedral is no easy thing ;
several of the pilgrims gave it up. Fearless as
usual, Céline and Teresa, leaving the timid ones

behind, pressed on till, with the small group of
bolder pilgrims, they arrived at the top.

From Milan the pilgrims made their way to
Venice. To Teresa it was a city full of charm,
but also full of sadness. She was more interested
in the awful dungeons, where prisoners were
kept in old days, even than in the splendid
palace of the Doges. Thinking of this visit some
years afterwards, she says : ' While visiting these
dreadful prisons I fancied myself in the times of
the Martyrs. Gladly would I have chosen this
dark abode for my dwelling if there had been any
question of confessing my faith.'

It was night when they left for Rome. Teresa
was asleep when they arrived there and was
awakened by the porters calling ' Roma.' The
pilgrims took up the cry : ' Roma, Roma,'
echoed through the train. At last she knew it was
no dream, she was really in the Holy City, the
City of Rome.

No city makes so varied an appeal as Rome,
with her old pagan monuments reaching far
back into history before Christianity came, the
ancient churches, the splendid palaces, the city's
own natural beauty. All this attracts people of
the most different kind.

It was not these, nor even the splendour of
St. Peter's, that most thrilled Teresa ; it was the
Colosseum—a pagan monument indeed, but far
more wonderful than its pagan grandeur is the
fact that here is the place where, more than any

other, the early Martyrs shed their blood for Christ. The Colosseum was the ancient Roman theatre, in which the Christians were thrown to the lions in thousands. It is very old and, when Teresa saw it, it had not been restored as it is now. It was a ruin of the past and a very dangerous one with its overhanging walls in the old passages. To get down to the centre of this great theatre, to the spot where the Martyrs died, was very perilous and strictly forbidden. This did not daunt Teresa. She saw a path down and, disregarding the warning of the guide, said to Céline : ' Come, follow quickly, we shall be able to get through.' They both hurried down, scrambling over the ruins which crumbled under their feet. Their father, astonished at their boldness, called out, but they did not listen. They found the spot, marked with a Cross, where the Martyrs had died. They both fell on their knees and kissed the ground which, hundreds of years before, had been reddened by the blood of Christians. ' I prayed,' says Teresa, ' for the grace to be a martyr for Jesus, and I felt in the depths of my heart that my prayer was heard.'

From the Colosseum the pilgrims went to the Catacombs. The Catacombs are the underground cemeteries where the Christian Martyrs were buried and where the Mass was said in secret when persecution made it dangerous to say Mass in either the churches or the houses

of the faithful. Among the tombs there was one
above all the others which little Teresa was bent
on finding and could not rest content till it was
found. This was the tomb of the girl martyr,
St. Cecilia, the young Roman Society girl who
converted her young husband and his friend and
led them both to the glory of martyrdom. Her
story had always been a favourite one with Teresa.
At last she saw where this girl's martyred body
had lain. She could not resist the impulse to
lie down in the tomb where that body had
rested.

Now came the most important day of all.
Milan, Venice, even the Colosseum, wonderful
though they were, were but little to Teresa
compared with what was, in her mind, the main
object of the pilgrimage ; that was the visit to
the Holy Father and the chance it would give
her of winning his permission to enter Carmel at
the age of fifteen. When the day came, November
20, they went in the early morning to the Vatican.
At eight o'clock they assisted at the Holy Father's
Mass. The reverence with which the Holy
Father said Mass made a deep impression on the
child. She noticed that the Gospel for the day
contained the words : ' Fear not, little flock, it
hath pleased your Father to give you a kingdom.'
This gave her confidence. She says : ' I would
not fear. I would trust that the kingdom of
Carmel would soon be mine.'

After offering the Holy Sacrifice Leo XIII

went to his seat in the great hall to receive the pilgrims. Each person was presented in turn. This was the great moment. Here was the Holy Father surrounded by many high dignitaries. On either side were standing many monsignori and other prelates ; in the background were the Noble Guard with their splendid uniforms. With over a hundred pilgrims listening, could this child of fourteen and a half possibly have the courage to ask the Pope to do for her what her own Bishop had refused to do ? The Monsignor who was introducing the pilgrims came from Lisieux and knew little Teresa. When he saw her and Céline approach the Holy Father to be presented he announced in a loud voice that nobody was to speak to His Holiness. Teresa looked imploringly for a sign from Céline. ' Speak,' said the elder sister. In a moment Teresa is at the feet of Leo XIII. Quickly she kisses the Pontiff's foot and grasps the hand which he holds out to her ; then, with eyes filled with tears, in dead silence so that everyone could hear her faltering voice, she exclaims : ' Most Holy Father, I have a great favour to ask.' The Pope bent down his head till it touched Teresa's veil and his dark, piercing eyes sought to read those of the child. She continued : ' Most Holy Father, in honour of your Jubilee allow me to enter Carmel at fifteen.' Here the Monsignor intervened. ' Most Holy Father,' he said, ' this is a child who desires the life of Carmel. The

Superiors are at the moment considering the question.' ' Well, well, my child,' said the Pope, ' do whatever the Superiors shall decide.' Clasping her hands and resting them on his knees, little Teresa makes her last despairing appeal : ' Oh, Holy Father, if only you say Yes everyone else will agree.' The Pope, gazing at her intently, said in an earnest voice : ' Well, well, my child, you will enter if it be God's Will.' The other pilgrims were waiting their turn ; Teresa was about to speak again, but one of the Noble Guard told her to rise. As she still remained kneeling they took her by the arms, and the Monsignor had to come to their aid before she would leave her place at the Holy Father's feet. Just as they compelled her to rise the Holy Father laid his hand on her lips, then lifted it to bless her, following her with his eyes for quite a long time.

It was over. The long weary journey to Rome had apparently failed in its object. The poor child went away crying bitterly. She had done all in her power to answer Heaven's call. Almighty God thought it best to disappoint her. It was a very hard trial for little Teresa.

The pilgrims returned to Lisieux. As soon as she got back Teresa went to the Convent to tell her sisters what had happened. Pauline, now Sister Agnes, who had always encouraged her, said : ' Why don't you write to the Bishop? For he has not sent you the written answer he promised you.' Teresa did this, but the Bishop remained silent.

It seemed indeed as though God was not going to allow Teresa's great longing to be fulfilled. But in spite of that she tells us that, through all her tears, she was at peace.

And then, on the first day of the year, 1888, the post brought her a letter. It was from the Prioress with the good news that the Bishop had given his permission for her to enter Carmel, but that the Prioress had decided it would be wiser to put it off till after Lent.

She spent the months that remained in preparing for the great day. April 9 was the day chosen.

The evening before, the whole family—her father and her two sisters who were still at home, her uncle and aunt and their two little girls, one of whom was later to enter Carmel—were all gathered in the little home Teresa loved so dearly. Everything in it was precious to her ; the garden where they had played, the hearth round which they had spent so many winter evenings, all called to her heart. But far more than this she felt the separation from the people she loved so much and whom she must leave. In her own words : 'Just when one would rather be forgotten, words of the deepest tenderness were on all lips, so as to make the sacrifice of separation more keenly felt than ever.'

The following morning the family assisted at

Mass. When Mass was over Teresa walked to the cloister door. Those around her were crying, yet she shed no tears, but, as she tells us, ' My heart beat so violently that I asked myself whether I was not about to die.' She knelt to receive her father's blessing. Then she entered the open door and crossed the threshold of Carmel. The desire of her heroic heart was fulfilled at last. She tells us, ' The doors of Carmel closed behind me, and there I received the embraces of the two sisters who had each been a mother to me, and of a new family whose loving devotedness is unknown to the world.'

The first part of the story of little Teresa's life is over. During it all, from the first days at Alençon to the final appeal to the Holy Father in Rome, it is always the same little person we see, loving and determined. The determined yet loving baby at Alençon ; the loyal little friend at school, who never gave up praying for the friend who had forgotten her ; the loving little daughter, yet brave enough to break her father's heart by asking him to let her leave him ; the intrepid little climber in the Cathedral at Milan, who yet had the understanding sympathy to see that the sadness of Venice was greater than all its splendour ; the frail, yet daring venturer into the Colosseum, a true companion to the frail girl martyr, St. Cecilia ; finally, the courageous little girl of fourteen and a half whose faltering voice was heard in the Vatican, making her appeal in the hearing of hundreds of listeners to the Pope. Such was the character of Teresa. Such it will remain, as we shall see, all through her life in Carmel till she goes to Heaven.

Loving and determined, tenderly devoted to her home and family yet even more devoted to Our Blessed Lord and determined to prove her love for Him to the utmost no matter what it might cost her or the family whom she loved so dearly.

CHAPTER THREE

ST. TERESA IN CARMEL

EVERYTHING in the convent delighted
Teresa, especially her little cell with its
bare boards, its straw mattress and simple bed,
its little bench and hour-glass. She tells us what
peace came over her soul and with what untold
joy she kept repeating to herself : ' Now I am
here for ever.'

Why was this clever, beautiful girl of fifteen,
who had such a deep appreciation of life, so
radiantly happy at being shut up in Carmel,
living in a bare convent cell ? It was because
there are certain people whom Our Lord calls,
to love Him and to help Him in the work of
saving souls, in a special manner. He calls them
to do it by prayer and sacrifice. In a Carmelite
convent every hour is arranged so as to give as
much time as possible to prayer, and the life is
ordered so as to give as many opportunities as
possible for sacrifice. By their prayer the Carmelite nuns are drawn as close as is possible on
this earth to the Sacrifice of Our Lord on the
Cross, and thus they are able, in a special way,
to offer all their sacrifices with His, thus bringing

down blessings upon other souls, so that these souls may give up sin and selfishness, draw near to the Cross and love Our Blessed Lord. In order that, undisturbed, they may give their whole life to loving and serving Our Lord in this way, the Carmelites are completely separated from the world and live what is called an enclosed life.

St. Teresa said : ' There is only one thing to do here below, to love Jesus and to save souls so that they may love Him too.' She entered Carmel because she knew she was called to do this by prayer and sacrifice.

THE POSTULANT

For the first year Teresa was a postulant. This word means someone who is asking to be allowed to join the Order. During this time the nuns have to test the reality of her Vocation in order to see if she should be allowed to become a novice, which is the second stage of preparation in the life of Carmel. From her very entrance Teresa found the life full of sacrifice.

She had been brought up in a comfortable home. In Carmel there were no bodily comforts. Her dress which she wore as a postulant was severely plain and simple, and was soon to be followed by the coarse and rough habit of the Carmelite Order : she had to sweep and clean the refectory, the passages and stairs and to take her place in the laundry and kitchen. There was practically no heating in Carmel, and later on the long winters were going to try Teresa very severely. There was only one fire and, after having allowed herself but a few minutes to get warmed by it, she would have to cross an open cloister to reach her cell and often she was too cold to sleep at all.

St. Teresa, at first, was not good at housework. On one occasion, when she had left a cobweb in the cloister, the Mother Prioress said to her before the whole community : ' It is easy to see that we have a child of fifteen to sweep our cloister.' It may seem to us that the Mother Prioress was over-severe in humiliating Teresa in public in this manner ; but to live the life of Carmel it is necessary to make a complete surrender of pride and self-love, and to test the readiness of Teresa to do this was one of the duties of her superiors. Just because the Mother Prioress realized that Teresa was of such special metal she treated her even more strictly than was usual. Another reason for the Mother Prioress being strict was that Teresa, being an attractive and affectionate child of fifteen, might so very easily have become the spoilt child of the community. This the Mother Prioress was determined to avoid at all costs. Later on Teresa tells us how grateful she was for this, because, as she says, her heart, ' so carefully guarded in the world, might have so easily been ensnared by human affection in the Cloister.' She tells us how, in fact, when she was a postulant, she was continually tempted to find little excuses for asking permission to see her Mother Prioress, really in order to give herself the pleasure of talking with her, and how sometimes this temptation was so strong that she had to hurry past the Mother Prioress' cell and cling to the banisters to keep herself from turning back.

This shows us that Teresa in Carmel had the same loving, affectionate nature as in Les Buissonnets, but was still as determined as ever that her heart, which had sacrificed the companionships of home, should still be completely given to God in the Cloister.

St. Teresa came to Carmel to love Our Lord through prayer and sacrifice. Our Lord led her to Himself by this path right up to the day of her Clothing.

The day of her Clothing is a great day for a Carmelite nun. On that day the community accepts her as a novice, she enters into her second stage of trial, and on this day the postulant definitely gives up the world to become the spouse of Christ. The ceremony, therefore, has the appearance of a wedding. The postulant enters the chapel dressed as a bride and then, after the service, puts aside her bridal clothes for the coarse habit of the community.

On the day of her Clothing, St. Teresa's father, who had, contrary to all expectations, recovered from a second attack of paralysis, gave his arm to his daughter while together they made their solemn entry into the public chapel. Teresa was wearing a bridal dress of white velvet covered with rich Alençon lace such as her mother used to make. This lace dress can be seen in the Hall of Relics near by. The velvet was used in the cloth-of-gold vestments worn during the ceremonies in the Carmel chapel after her Beatification. At the close of the ceremony in the chapel Teresa said good-bye to her father at the threshold of the Cloister. On entering, she tells us that her eyes fell first of all on the statue of the Holy Child ' smiling at me amid flowers and lights.' To tend this statue was to be her special duty later. Then, turning towards the quadrangle, she saw with delight that it was covered with snow. St. Teresa had a great love for snow. She had specially desired that there should be snow on her Clothing day, but, as the weather was so mild, she had given up all hope of this. The incident was ever afterwards spoken of as the ' little miracle ' of her Clothing.

Teresa is now a Novice

The novitiate is intended to be a time of progress in self-conquest. St. Teresa had many battles with herself, and at first, as she tells us, she found them very hard. When she was sacristan it was her duty to put the keys of the Communion grating back in the Mother Prioress' room. This gave her a chance of seeing the Mother Prioress which was very precious to her. One morning, during a time when the Mother Prioress was ill, another sister feared St. Teresa might wake her and suggested that she herself had better put back the keys. St. Teresa told her quietly that she was just as anxious as herself that there should be no noise, adding that it was her duty to return the keys, and attempted to enter the room. The noise they made awoke the Mother Prioress, and the other sister made a lengthy story, putting the blame on St. Teresa. St. Teresa was burning to defend herself when it occurred to her that, if she did, she would only lose her peace of mind and, knowing that she had not sufficient virtue to keep silence when accused, she took refuge in flight. The struggle was so violent that she had to sit on the stairs to calm herself down.

The most difficult thing to overcome, we all know, is our pride. The surest way to overcome it is to realize that humiliations are most precious, just because they touch our self-love more than anything else. It is the task of the novice mistress to help her novices as much as she possibly can to learn this great lesson. One day it happened that a small jar, which had been left by a window, was found broken. Believing that St. Teresa was the culprit, the novice mistress reproached her for leaving it about, adding that she was most untidy and must be more careful in future. Although St. Teresa was in no way to blame she refrained from saying a word in self-defence and merely promised to be more orderly in future.

Her novitiate passed quietly except for the great sorrow of her father's illness. The great suffering did more than anything else had done for the perfection of St. Teresa's soul, teaching her to surrender herself to the Will of God and to find in it her joy and peace even when it cost her most.

She spent her days in little hidden acts of kindness, such as folding the mantles which the sisters had forgotten and being ready to help them in every possible way.

Physical penances and bodily mortifications were forbidden to St. Teresa because she was too young. This made her give her whole devotion to the overcoming of her pride and self-love, which was far better for her than any bodily penance.

Yet one more humiliation awaited St. Teresa before she was allowed to make her solemn Profession, that is to say to take her final vows. At the close of her year of novitiate the Mother Prioress called her to her and told her that the Superior of the Carmel had forbidden her to make her Profession and take her final vows for another eight months. At first St. Teresa found this sacrifice very hard to accept, but she soon realized that she already belonged to Our Lord and had given herself entirely to Him, so that the actual ceremony merely confirmed what was already true. This gave her patience and, remembering that a bride desires to make herself as beautiful as possible for her bridegroom, she asked Our Lady to help her to make a wedding dress—that is to say, a soul adorned with every kind of virtue, so that nothing should be wanting when the day of her Profession did come.

At last the day arrived, September 8, 1890. The evening before, her soul was swept by a storm of temptation. The devil did his utmost to persuade her that she had no vocation and that she must return to the world. It is impossible to describe the suffering St. Teresa went through. What was she to do ? Happily she chose the right course and decided to tell the novice mistress without a moment's delay. The latter, laughing at her fears, completely reassured her. Next morning, with her soul flooded with joy and peace, a peace which she says never left her afterwards, she pronounced her vows. Next to her heart she bore a slip of paper on which was written : 'I offer myself to Thee, O my Beloved, that Thou mayest perfectly accomplish Thy Will in me.'

St. Teresa has now taken her final vows and has given herself in Carmel completely to Our

Lord. She stands at the threshold of her career
as a nun. What is the career of a nun? It is
holiness. Teresa's one desire was to be a saint.
To Teresa being a saint meant loving Almighty
God with all her heart and soul and winning
others by her love so that they might love Him
too. She chose the life of prayer and sacrifice
in Carmel because it was to her the most complete
way of doing this.

Teresa tells us that, at the beginning of her
life as a Carmelite nun, when she thought of
her weakness and her failings and then thought
of holiness it seemed to her that holiness was like
a great mountain and that she was only a grain
of sand, so far away did holiness seem. She
asked Our Lord therefore to show her a way to
holiness which would be little and simple, for
she could do nothing wonderful or great. One
day she opened her Gospels and came across the
scene where the Apostles had been arguing who
should be greatest in the Kingdom of Heaven.
Our Lord calls them round Him and, taking a
little child in His arms, He says to His Apostles :
' Unless you be converted and become as little
children you shall not enter the kingdom of
heaven. Whosoever shall humble himself as
this little child, the same is the greater in the
kingdom of heaven.' Filled with joy, Teresa
said to herself : Here is my Little Way. Jesus
tells me that to enter the Kingdom of Heaven
I must become as a little child. I know I can

do nothing great, but I can try and become little ; and if only I become little enough Jesus will take me in His arms and lift me up to heights of holiness which by myself I could never reach.

Teresa then asked herself what exactly did Jesus mean ? What must she do to become as a little child ? As she thought this over she saw quite clearly that if she was to become as a little child, then she must look upon God as her Father and she must treat her Father in Heaven just as a little child treats its father on earth. That is why she called her Little Way the Little Way of Spiritual Childhood.

This means three very important things. First, to a little child its father is not someone far away, someone whom it hardly ever sees and of whom it is afraid. On the contrary the father is someone who is very close to his little child, someone who is very dear, of whom the little child is not afraid but whom it loves, because it knows that he loves it and wants its love.

To St. Teresa, therefore, Almighty God was not someone far away, but her own Father, always with her, watching over her closely and loving her tenderly, someone whom she loved with all her heart because she knew He loved her and wanted her to love Him.

Secondly, the little child, just because it is little, can do nothing by itself. If it lets go its father's hand it falls to the ground and is helpless, but if only it holds its father's hand tight, then it is able to go exactly where the father wishes it to go—up stairs or through dark passages—which by itself it simply could not do. It depends upon its father for everything. Teresa never forgot that it was exactly the same between her and her Father in Heaven ; without Him she could do nothing. If she was to become a saint she must put her hand in His, surrender her will entirely to His Will and follow Him wherever He led her. The one thing she dreaded was that her Little Way should be a little way of her own, the way of pride and self-will, and not the way of her Father in Heaven, the way of humble dependence and complete obedience. So she determined that she would always, at all costs, remain very little so that her Heavenly Father could lead her exactly where He wished.

Thirdly, a little child, just because it does not trust in itself but puts its hand in its father's hand and trusts entirely to him, is completely confident. It knows that, with its father, it is always safe because its father loves it. The smaller it is the more sure it is of this.

In the same way St. Teresa, just because she was utterly dependent upon her Father and never trusted in herself, had perfect trust in Him. She knew that He would never take her anywhere that was not absolutely safe, however difficult the way might seem and however much at times she might be hurt. She knew it was safe because it was chosen not by her but by Him Who loved her so dearly.. Therefore St. Teresa was always radiantly happy and always at peace. Nothing could disturb her complete trust in her Father.

CHAPTER FOUR

THE LITTLE WAY, THE WAY OF THE CROSS

' UNLESS you be converted and become as little children, you shall not enter the kingdom of heaven.' These words were spoken by Our Blessed Lord. But He also said : ' If any man will come after me, let him deny himself, and take up his cross daily, and follow me.' The Little Way of Spiritual Childhood, therefore, is the Way of the Cross, for unless we take up our cross we cannot follow Our Lord Jesus Christ. The Little Way is the way of the Cross because it is the way of love ; and the way of love is the way of sacrifice. It is the way our Heavenly Father chose for His Son, it is the way He chooses for all of us, His little children. To tread this Little Way means to forget ourselves completely, to sacrifice our own will and our own desires. It means to love one another as Jesus has loved us.

St. Teresa's life in Carmel was just that. All day long she made it her one object to love her sisters in the community as Jesus loved them. Jesus had laid down His life for them. She would lay down her life for them too. She would show her love in the only way little children can show their love, that is by little things, by little acts of unselfish love all day long. At every moment she would forget herself and have just one thought : What is it that my sister wants ? What can I do for her ? Every little sacrifice, every interruption, every tiresome duty was to her a treasure because she could offer it to her Heavenly Father as a proof of her love for Him and for her sisters in Carmel who were His children too. There was nothing weak in St. Teresa's love for her sisters. On the contrary to Teresa love meant a fearless loyalty to truth. At one period of her life in Carmel she and another sister were thrown much together and were allowed to talk together on spiritual subjects. This sister was many years older than St. Teresa. As time went on the other began to talk about her great devotion to the Mother Prioress. St. Teresa realized that this was wrong. She knew she must either speak out fearlessly or stop the talks entirely. She decided to speak out. This she found very difficult as her companion was so much older than herself. She told her that her conversation was wrong and that her love for the Mother Prioress was really self-love because in it she was seeking her own pleasure. St. Teresa told her how, when she was a postulant, she had been tempted in this way and had found the temptation difficult to overcome. The nun was won completely by

St. Teresa's straightforwardness and simplicity, and all was well.

But St. Teresa did not think only of Carmel. She thought of the whole world. She thought of the Catholic Church in every country, of the missionaries toiling in far-off lands. She thought also of all those children of her Heavenly Father outside the Church and of all those who neither knew Him nor cared about Him. For all these all day long she would give her life. And here again it was by little things, little prayers, little sacrifices. All her hidden sacrifices and disappointments, all her little joys and consolations, above all her sufferings of whatever kind, especially those that were hidden, she offered daily to Our Blessed Lord to show her love for Him and the souls for whom He died. She offered them to Him, asking Him to take them, to unite them to His Cross and to use them for winning all the world to love Him as He wanted it to do. Thus suffering became the great means by which St. Teresa drew near to Jesus and shared His Cross, and so entered into the deepest secret of His Love for her and for other souls.

And all the time she remained a little child, loving, humble, trustful, surrendering herself into her Father's arms, so that He carried her along the Little Way of Spiritual Childhood, through sacrifice and suffering, through darkness and trial, straight into Heaven. Thus did little Teresa become the great saint that she is to-day.

Little Teresa was carried along the Little Way of Spiritual Childhood through sacrifice and suffering because she surrendered herself so completely and with such loving childlike trust into her Heavenly Father's arms. All the sacrifice and suffering which came to her in her Little Way she knew to be the result of her Heavenly Father's love for her. She knew that it was given to her by Him so that through it she might be purified from all self-love and give Him a more perfect love and so be more completely united to Him. At the same time she knew that it was given her in order that she might offer Him for other souls and so win the love of these other souls for her Heavenly Father too.

It was all the work of the Merciful Love of God stooping down to His little children and lifting them into the closest possible communion with Himself. It was just Our Heavenly Father longing to pour out His love into the souls of His children whose love He so desired.

St. Teresa's one desire was to respond with every power in her being. She would offer herself completely to the workings of this Merciful Love so that she might give Him the love which He so desired and might win for Him the love of countless of His other children. She would be a victim of the Merciful Love. She made her act of offering as a victim to the Merciful Love of God on June 9, 1895. She tells us herself how she was led to make this offering.

' In the year 1895 I received the grace to understand better than ever how much Jesus desires to be loved. While thinking one day of those who offer themselves as victims to the Justice of God, and who turn aside the punishment due to sinners, taking it upon themselves, I felt such an offering to be both noble and generous. I was very far, nevertheless, from feeling myself drawn to make it, and from the depths of my heart I cried : " O, my Divine Master, shall Thy justice alone find atoning victims ? Has not Thy Merciful Love need of them also ? On every side it is ignored and rejected . . . those hearts on which Thou wouldst lavish it turn to creatures and seek their happiness in the miserable satisfaction of a moment rather than cast themselves into Thy arms—into the sweet furnace of Thy infinite Love.

' " O my God, must that love which is disdained lie hidden in Thy Heart ? It seems to me that if Thou shouldst find souls offering themselves as a holocaust to Thy Love, Thou wouldst consume them rapidly and wouldst be pleased to set free those flames of infinite tenderness now imprisoned in Thy Heart. If Thy Justice which avenges itself upon earth must needs be satisfied, how much more must Thy Merciful Love desire to inflame souls, since ' Thy Mercy reacheth even to the very Heavens.' O Jesus, permit that I may be that happy victim—consume Thy holocaust with the fire of Divine Love." '

Thus did St. Teresa make her offering. From that moment onwards her life became one continual offering of herself to the Merciful Love of God, through little sacrifices all day long by which she grew in love towards her Heavenly Father and to her sisters in Carmel and by which she also won for her Heavenly Father the love of countless souls in the world outside.

We have said that St. Teresa put her Little Way into practice through little things, little acts of love and sacrifice for those around her. We will now watch her as she moves along her path. We are able to do so because one day after recreation, when Teresa had been recalling the memories of her childhood, her eldest sister Marie, vividly impressed by the charming manner in which Teresa had expressed them, asked Mother Agnes, then Prioress, to command St. Teresa to write these memories down. Sister Marie was anxious to preserve them for herself and her sisters. At first Mother Agnes refused; finally, however, she yielded to Sister Marie's entreaties and gave Teresa the order to write them down. Teresa obeyed at once.

Before Teresa began to write she knelt in front of the statue of Our Lady which had given her so many proofs of her heavenly mother's care. As she knelt she begged that dear Mother to guide her hand and to ensure that only what was pleasing to her should find place there.

We can only take one or two examples which she

gives us of how she tried in her simple way to love her sisters as Jesus loved them. We shall notice how, in every case, it is always through little things, things just like those which we all meet in our ordinary lives.

There was in the convent a certain nun who got on Sister Teresa's nerves in everything she did. ' It must have been the devil,' Teresa says, ' who made me see so many disagreeable points in her.' Whenever she met her Teresa wanted to go round the other way to avoid her. She knew, however, that this would not do. So she determined to overcome her own feelings and deliberately set to work to do as much as she possibly could for her, even though tempted to be disagreeable, and always she did it with a smile. At last one day the nun turned to her and said : ' Tell me, Sœur Thérèse, what is it in me that attracts you so ? I never meet you without being welcomed by a most gracious smile.'

Another sister, by name Sister St. Peter, was a great invalid, and someone had to leave the evening meditation at ten minutes to six to take her to the refectory. Knowing the difficulty of pleasing the poor invalid, it cost St. Teresa a great effort to offer her services ; but she did so. Her help was accepted, though only after considerable persuasion. Every evening when Teresa saw her shake her hour-glass she knew it was the signal to start. Summoning up all her courage, Teresa rose and the little ceremony began. First her stool had to be moved and carried in a particular way without the least hurry. Then began the journey. Supporting the poor old sister by her girdle, she tried to perform her task as gently as she could. If by chance the sister stumbled Teresa was told that she was going too fast and that she would certainly make her fall. When Teresa tried to lead her more slowly she would say : ' Where are you ? . . . I don't feel your hand. . . . You are letting go your hold. . . . I am going to fall. . . . I was right when I said you were too young to take care of me.' At last they reached the refectory without further mishap. There fresh difficulties awaited them. Taking every care not to hurt the poor old nun, Teresa had to install her, with some manœuvring, in her place. That done, she had to turn back her sleeves—always according to her own special rubric—and then Teresa was free to go. Noticing, however, that it was with extreme difficulty that she cut her bread, Teresa would not leave her till she had done this for her. As the invalid had never expressed any wish that she should do this the little kindness touched her greatly. Through this little incident, and still more perhaps through always appearing very glad to do it, she won the old sister's entire confidence. One cold winter evening, when Teresa was humbly leading Sister St. Peter, there suddenly fell on her ear a strain of distant music. There rose before her the picture of a richly furnished room, brilliantly lighted and decorated, full of elegantly dressed young men and women talking together as is the way of the world. Then she turned to the poor old invalid. Instead of sweet music she heard only her complaints ; instead of rich gilding she saw the bare dark walls of the Cloister, scarcely visible in the dim light. Teresa tells us that not for a thousand years of such worldly pleasures, as she had suddenly seen in imagination, would she have exchanged that ten minutes spent in her little act of kindness to poor Sister St. Peter. For Our Lord had said : ' Inasmuch as you have done it to one of the least of these, my brethren, you have done it unto me.'

For a long time Teresa's place at meditation was near a sister who fidgeted incessantly either with her rosary or something else. Teresa was extremely sensitive to any sort of noise and was tried beyond words by the irritating rattle. She was strongly tempted to turn round and with one glance to silence the offender. But in her heart she knew that she ought to bear with her patiently, for the love of God first of all, also to avoid giving her pain, and above all because it was not her duty to reprove her. She therefore remained quiet, but the effort cost her so much that she was bathed in perspiration. Knowing, however, that this was not enough, she determined to find peace by actually taking pleasure in the disagreeable noise. So instead of vainly attempting not to hear it she set herself to listen to it attentively as though it were delightful music, and so she passed her meditation in offering this music to Our Lord.

These three incidents are typical of how Teresa used the simplest little things as instruments whereby to prove her love for Our Blessed Lord and for her sisters for whom He died. Above all they show us St. Teresa transforming the little disagreeables which are so difficult to bear into blessings both of her own soul and for the souls of those around her. This in reality is the mark of holiness, not just to bear with our little miseries, but joyfully to transform them to blessings.

So St. Teresa passed along her Little Way, unnoticed by most of the community. A few only realized something of what was going on. During her last illness two lay sisters were talking once about Teresa, and one said to the other: ' Sister Teresa is soon going to die. Whatever will Mother Prioress have to say about her after she is gone ? For this little sister, charming though she is, has really done nothing worth talking about.'

Through all this St. Teresa's aim had been to remain ordinary and hidden. She did not wish that anyone should notice either what she did or what she suffered. ' Unknown to anyone,' she says, ' this was the path I trod for fully five years. It was precisely the flower I wished to offer to Jesus, a hidden flower which keeps its perfume for Him alone.' In spite of this she was always cheerful and full of fun. When some duty kept her from recreation the sisters were often heard to say : ' We shall have no fun to-day, for Teresa is not going to be here.' ' God likes a smiling soul.' So said St. Teresa. One of her favourite saints was Blessed Théophane Venard, and the reason was because he was always merry and joyful.

St. Teresa's little acts of love were not confined to Carmel. She had always hoped that she would get well enough to be able to go to the Carmel of Saigon, in Indo-China. She never was able to do this, but the mission field was always in her mind. She told her sister that, when she died, she hoped that money would not be spent on wreaths for her, but that it should be given to the missions in foreign lands. At the beginning of her last illness, when she was able to walk, though only with great difficulty, she was in the garden when one of the sisters said to her : ' You should not be out here. Walking is not good for you, for it is too tiring.' She replied : ' Yes, I know, but then you see I am happy to offer every step that wearies me for the sake of missionaries who are worn out with their work among the heathen.' Another time, when they were persuading her to take remedies which she knew were useless, she said : ' These remedies will never cure me, but I have arranged with God that they shall go to the profit of the poor missionaries, who have neither the time nor the means to take care of themselves. I have asked God to use all the care that is bestowed on me to cure them.'

Now the moment has come when Almighty God having taught the Little Way of Spiritual Childhood to little Teresa is going through her to teach it to other souls. Her rapid advance in the practice of virtue and in holiness could not remain altogether hidden and in February, 1893, Teresa was appointed to assist Mother Gonzaga who was then Novice Mistress. In effect this meant that Teresa was Novice Mistress without the title, for the formation of the Novices was left almost entirely in her hands. To have all the work of Novice Mistress without the title exactly suited Teresa who always desired to be hidden in all she did. Less than six months after her appointment her sister Céline, the playmate of her childhood days, entered Carmel. We can imagine the joy it must have been to Teresa to have among the first novices to whom she was to teach her Little Way that sister whom she afterwards spoke of as ' the sweet echo of my soul.'

The moment the task was entrusted to her she realized it was beyond her powers, instinctively she flung herself into God's arms. ' Convinced

that I could do nothing by myself my task
appeared simpler. I strove solely to unite myself
more and more to God, knowing that everything
else would be given me abundantly—never has
my trust been deceived. As often as nourishment
has been required for the souls entrusted to me
I have found my hand full.'

With her deep spiritual insight she realized
at once the delicacy of her task. ' From afar,'
she says, ' it seems easy to do good to souls, to
make them love God more, to mould them
according to our own ideas and views. But
coming closer, we find on the contrary that to do
good without God's help is as impossible as to
bring back the sun during the night. We feel
that we must absolutely forget our own tastes,
our personal ideas and guide souls, not by our
way, but by the particular path which Jesus
points out. And this is not the chief difficulty.
What cost me most is being obliged to observe
every fault and slightest imperfection and to
wage deadly war against them.'

As Novice Mistress St. Teresa is the same as
we saw her to be as a little girl, loving and
determined. She was infinitely loving and understanding. A novice once came to beg her pardon
for a fault, Teresa replied : ' If you but knew
what I feel ! I have never before understood so
well the love with which Jesus receives us when
we ask His pardon for a fault. If I, His poor little
creature, feel so much tenderness towards you

the moment you return to me what must pass in the Heart of God when we return to Him.'

At the same time when necessary she was equally determined. ' With souls under our direction we must speak truthfully what we think. I always act thus. If I am not liked what matter ! Besides I do not seek for that. Let them not come to me if they do not wish to be told the entire truth.'

In this spirit she trained her novices in the Little Way of spiritual childhood.

' Tell us,' they asked her on one occasion, ' what we must do to be *as little children*. What do you mean by *keeping little ?* '

She answered : ' When we keep little we recognize our own nothingness and expect everything from the goodness of God, exactly as a little child expects everything from its father. Nothing worries us ! Even among the very poor a little child is always given what he needs. . . . Again, being as a little child with God means that we do not attribute to ourselves the virtues we may possess in the belief that we are capable of something. It implies, on the contrary, our recognition of the fact that God places the treasure of virtue in the hand of his little child for him to use as he needs it, though all the while it is God's treasure. Finally, to *keep little* means not to lose courage at the sight of one fault. Little children often tumble, but they are too small to suffer injury.'

Her first novices, who found some difficulty in understanding her, were soon followed by souls more open and more generous by nature, who did not hesitate to go forward gladly on the path she pointed out to them. This marked the beginning of a period of special fervour in the Carmel at Lisieux which was never afterwards to know relaxation. To-day that same Carmel radiates the Little Way of Spiritual Childhood to all the Catholic world, that Little Way which first was taught by St. Teresa to the little novitiate within its humble walls.

Thus did Teresa become the teacher of her Little Way to others. It was, as we can all see, the way of the Child Jesus at Nazareth. It was at Nazareth that the Little Way first was lived, the Little Way of Love, Humility and Trust—little because of the little things which formed its setting. The Child Jesus showed His love to God the Father, to His Mother and to St. Joseph through little acts of love and sacrifice.

St. Teresa was given the name of Teresa of the Child Jesus, a name she had always hoped for because of her devotion to the Little Jesus of Bethlehem. Her very name then recalls Nazareth and the Holy Child. Nazareth was the inspiration of her Little Way, sure and safe in its simplicity. The Little way is the way of Nazareth, therefore it is the way of Our Lady. St. Teresa and Our Lady are inseparable.

After her Divine Son, Our Lady is the most

perfect model of all those simple virtues which make up ordinary life. Our Blessed Lady is indeed Queen of Heaven and her glory is greater than the glory of the Saints. But to Teresa there was something greater still—Our Lady was her Mother. ' O, how I love Our Lady,' she said, ' she is more Mother than Queen.' The Mother of Nazareth, leading her children along the path of ordinary and hidden virtue, guides them securely along the Little Way of love, humility and trust, along which she herself walked hand in hand with the Child Jesus. The supreme privilege of a mother is not to be separated from her children or to outshine them, but to stoop down to them and share their life and especially share their pain. And so to St. Teresa the Mother of Nazareth, dear as she was, was dearer still as she became the Mother of Sorrows, sharing in the sorrow of her Child at the foot of His Cross, and therefore sharing at the same time in all the sorrow and suffering of her spiritual children down the ages.

St. Teresa was a perfect child of Mary. From her earliest days she loved her holy Mother, all through her life she clung to her hand and to her she turned, as we shall see, in her last moments.

' In prayer and sacrifice lies all my strength,' writes St. Teresa. We have seen her walking along the path of sacrifice. We will now watch her at her prayer.

The secret of the Little Way is to remain always

a little child. So the prayer of the Little Way will be the prayer of a little child, loving, humble and trustful because it knows it is loved by its Father and seeks to love Him in return. St. Teresa's prayer is therefore very simple. She prays with the simplicity of a little child. When little children wish to speak to their parents they do so in the simplest words. So St. Teresa did not make long prayers. She tells us so herself. ' Apart from the Divine Office which, in spite of my unworthiness, is a daily joy, I have not the courage to search through books for beautiful prayers. They are so numerous that it would only make my head ache. Besides each one is more lovely than the other. Unable, therefore, to say them all or to choose between them, I do as a little child would who cannot read ; I say just what I want to say to God quite simply and He never fails to understand.'

These words are full of the simple confidence of a little child. She just opens her heart and her Heavenly Father always understands. How did she know this ? Because she felt it ? Not always, for she prayed, as we shall see, often in the dark. We cannot go by feelings in our prayers. How then did she know it ? Because Our Lord had said so. ' Your Father knoweth that you have need of all these things.'

So many of us become discouraged with our prayers because we regard them as something long and wearying. Not so St. Teresa. ' To me,' she says, ' prayer is an uplifting of the heart, a glance towards Heaven, a cry of gratitude and love in times of sorrow as well as of joy.' Could anything be more simple ? At any moment of the day, whatever she is doing, whether she is sorrowful or happy, she looks up towards Heaven with a litle cry of gratitude and just says two words, ' Our Father.'

From the very first her prayer was mingled with sacrifice. Sometimes prayer was easy and Our Lord seemed near, but more often she did not find it easy to pray. St. Teresa did not mind this because she knew that Our Lord was only seeming to hide Himself from her in order that her prayer might be a more perfect act of faith, hope and love. She knew that faith is made perfect when things are hidden, hope is made perfect when all seems dark and love is made perfect through sacrifice. All this is to be found in St. Teresa's prayer.

When she found it very difficult to pray she didn't worry, but just did the best she could, however small it might seem to be. ' Thérèse,' she says in one of her letters, ' is far from the heights of fervour at this moment, but when I am in this state of spiritual dryness, unable to pray, or even to practise virtue, I look for little opportunities, for the smallest trifles, to please Jesus ; a smile or a kind word, for instance, when I would wish to be silent or to show that I am bored. If no such occasions offer, I try at least to say over and over again that I love Him. This is not hard, and it keeps alive the fire in my heart. Even should the fire of love seem dead, I would still throw my tiny straws on the ashes, and I am confident it would light up again. It is true I am not always faithful, but I never lose courage. I leave myself in the arms of Our Lord.' But to pray like this we, like St. Teresa, must be very little children, full of simple confidence.

St. Teresa entered Carmel in order to give her life to Our Blessed Lord in prayer and sacrifice, and so win other souls to love Him too. How could her prayers and her sacrifices have any power ? Only through the Sacrifice of the Cross. Our Lord's Sacrifice on the Cross is the one perfect sacrifice and the one perfect prayer. It is from her union with this Sacrifice that the Carmelite nun draws all her power.

The Mass is the continuation of Calvary ; therefore the Mass is the one perfect sacrifice, the one perfect prayer. It is the Mass then which is the centre of the life of Carmel, the source from which all its power is drawn. The Mass was the centre of St. Teresa's life ; she loved the Mass more than anything else on earth.

Just as when she was a tiny girl she would not be deterred by the rain, so in Carmel when she was very ill, towards the end of her life, and could hardly walk, she would slowly and with great pain make her way down the stairs to the chapel so that she should not miss Mass.

Our Blessed Lord, through an act of perfect prayer and sacrifice on the Cross, offered Himself the Victim of His Own Merciful Love for the whole world.

Now St. Teresa, through her Baptism, had been made one with Jesus, grafted on to Him, a living member of His Body. His Divine Life flowed in her like the sap which flows from the vine to all the branches. Because of this St. Teresa was able, in the Mass, to identify herself with Him in His Sacrifice, and so to make an offering of herself in union with Him and His Cross. Thus she was able, through the Mass, to let loose upon the world the torrents of grace which He won for us upon the Cross.

Here, and here alone, was it possible for her to make a perfect offering of herself to her Heavenly Father, for which she had come to Carmel. Here, and here alone, could she win other souls to love Him too. Here only, that is to say, could she fulfil the twofold purpose for which she had come to Carmel.

The heart of the Sacrifice of the Mass is the Divine Victim. In the Host St. Teresa saw the Perfect Victim of Love offering Himself to the Father, so winning for His Father's Love the souls of men. To her her Communion was simply receiving into her soul Him Who was this Perfect Victim of Love, so that through Him she might become a victim too.

It was through Jesus dwelling in her soul alone

that she could offer to her Heavenly Father a love
that was worthy of His Love ; and through Jesus
dwelling in her soul alone could she love her
sisters as He loved them. To be wholly consumed
by this love of her Father and of her sisters was her
whole desire. Through her Communion alone
what was otherwise impossible was made possible
for her. ' Oh, My Jesus, Thou dost never ask
what is impossible. Thou knowest better than
I how frail and imperfect I am. Thou knowest
that I shall never love my sisters as Thou hast
loved them unless Thou lovest them within me,
My Dearest Master. . . . When I show charity
to others I know it is Jesus acting within me,
and the more closely I am united to Him the
more truly I love my sisters.'

St. Teresa, all her life in Carmel, longed for
daily Communion, but it was not then the custom
of the Church even in religious houses. It was
not till later that Pope Pius X published his
decrees permitting daily Communion to all the
faithful and even to little children. On one
occasion, when influenza was raging in the
convent, she was left alone with two other sisters
to nurse the whole community. With her sisters
dying round her and in the midst of overwhelming
duties, she was allowed to make her Communion
every day. She writes of what a great joy it was
to have this privilege which, alas, was removed
again when the influenza had passed.

In her last illness she said that after her death

she would secure daily Communion for the convent ; and within fifteen days of her death, in the most unexpected manner, her prophecy came true.

Everything to do with the Blessed Sacrament was precious to her. When she was appointed sacristan she tells us what joy it was to her to be allowed to touch the sacred vessels and to clean and prepare them for the Mass.

To have been a priest would have been her greatest joy. ' Were I a priest, with what love, My Jesus, would I bear Thee in my hands when my words drew Thee down from Heaven ; with what love would I give Thee to the faithful.'

A simple, childlike devotion to the Blessed Sacrament is a mark of all those who tread the Little Way of Spiritual Childhood, a loving, grateful trust in this great gift which alone gives us the power to love our Heavenly Father and all those around us, in the way His children should.

CHAPTER FIVE

LAST DAYS

' I AM a child of Holy Church. My only glory
will be the reflection of the radiance that
streams from the brow of my mother the Church.'
Here we have the secret of St. Teresa's intense
love for the Church. ' Oh, how I love my mother
the Church,' she would say again and again.

The reason of this great love was because it
was her mother the Church alone who gave her
the power to become a saint. Her mother the
Church gave little Teresa the power to become a
saint because she nourished her with the very life
of God Himself, the life of supernatural grace
by which alone she could love God and become
like Him.

To St. Teresa her mother the Church existed
above all for one thing, to plant this supernatural love in her soul, to protect and develop it
until she became a saint.

We all possess this secret. We are all children
of our mother the Church. She plants the very
life of God in our souls at Baptism, strengthens it
at Confirmation, restores it in Confession should
we lose it, nourishes it in the Mass and in Holy

Communion and finally, with the Viaticum, she fortifies us with this life for our last journey. That is why, to St. Teresa, her mother the Church, from the Holy Father down to the last ordained priest, existed above all to plant in her soul this life of supernatural love.

Through her mother the Church she was one with all the other children throughout the world. From this sprang her great love for the missions and those labouring in them. They belonged to her and she belonged to them, because they were both children of the same mother. For her mother the Church and her children she will spend her life. 'All that I have, all is for the Church. I love my mother the Church and I bear in mind that the least act of pure love is of more value to her than all other works put together.'

It is through her mother the Church that she will offer her sacrifices all day long, her little expressions of her love ; and when she feels her weakness and her inability to do anything worth doing it is to her mother the Church in Heaven that she calls for assistance, that so her feeble efforts may extend beyond her little cell in Carmel to the whole Church on Earth and to the Church in Purgatory as well. 'Of what avail to Thee are my sacrifices, dear Jesus ? of what avail ? I know well that these petals of little price, these songs of love from a poor heart like mine, will nevertheless be pleasing to Thee.

They are but trifles, it is true, yet Thou wilt smile on them. The Church Triumphant, stooping towards her child, will gather up these scattered rose leaves and, placing them in Thy Divine Hands, so that they acquire an infinite value, will shower them on the Church Suffering to extinguish the flames and on the Church Militant to make her triumphant.' Thus will her mother the Church make her poor little acts of love, her little acts of sacrifice of infinite value.

To keep close to the heart of her mother in the Sacrifice of the Mass, at the very source of all supernatural love, and to be an instrument for giving that love to souls, this was the height of St. Teresa's ambition. ' Oh, Jesus, my Love, *my vocation is found at last.* I have found my place in the bosom of the Church ; and this place, O my God, Thou hast Thyself given to me ; in the heart of the Church my mother, I will be love.'

Our Heavenly Father wished St. Teresa to be our guide. He taught her the Little Way of Spiritual Childhood so that she might teach it to us. Most of us have to suffer, most of us have to be ill and all of us have to die before we can go to Heaven.

We are now going to see how Our Lord led little Teresa along the path of the Cross, through sickness and death, straight into Heaven. We shall see how all the time she was faithful to her

Little Way, how all through she was so completely the little child of her Heavenly Father, so completely surrendered to His Love that He was able to take her in His arms and carry her through suffering which she never could have borne by herself. We shall see how, by drawing her right into the mystery of His Cross, Our Lord perfected her love for Him and her power to win other souls to love Him too.

The first definite symptom that she was ill occurred just eighteen months before she actually died. It was a few minutes after midnight in the early morning of Good Friday, April 3, 1896. She tells us how she returned from watching at the Altar of Repose and how she had scarcely laid her head on the pillow when she had her first hæmorrhage. She immediately told the Prioress what had happened, but made so light of it that she was given permission to continue the life of the Carmel as usual.

It was not till a few months later that a hard, dry cough, which she could not hide, told everybody that little Teresa had consumption.

Her illness made rapid progress. In his efforts to prevent another hæmorrhage, the doctor gave her a painful course of treatment. Always smiling and patient, Teresa endured remedies which, at that time, were more painful than the illness itself.

For a few months she got better and the sisters hoped that she might recover, but all through the following winter she got gradually weaker. Towards Lent in 1897 very alarming symptoms showed themselves. The doctor continued his severe remedies, though with little hope of recovery. After each treatment Teresa had to remain very quiet for several hours.

At this time her Heavenly Father led His little child to suffer in another mysterious way. She received no comfort from her religion, but seemed to be always in the dark, unable to realize Our Lord's Presence with her. The thought of Heaven had no attraction for her and the devil tried his hardest to shake her faith.

St. Teresa was not daunted. She understood what her Heavenly Father was doing. He was giving her the opportunity of bearing all this and offering it for all those souls who, through their sin, were wandering in darkness and had lost their faith. ' Gladly,' she said, ' will I suffer thus if by so doing I can bring back one soul to the faith.'

At last Teresa became so ill that she had to leave her little cell and be taken to the infirmary. When she arrived in the infirmary her eyes fell on the statue of Our Lady. ' Why are you gazing at her so ? ' asked her sister. She replied : ' I have never seen her looking so beautiful as she is to-day. To-day it is the statue that is beautiful, but that other day when she smiled at me, as you well know, it was not the statue, it was herself.' So the blessed Mother who had come to her help in her first illness was to be her companion in her last.

Worn out with a continual cough and wasted with fever, she suffered greatly. The old doctor said to her sisters after one of his visits : ' If you only knew what this young nun is suffering —never have I seen such suffering borne with such supernatural joy.'

It was at about this moment in her illness that St. Teresa, whose life was so hidden, began to foretell things that would happen after her death, things which, at the moment, seemed entirely impossible but which, we shall see, were afterwards literally fulfilled.

One day her sister Marie said to her : ' What a sorrow it will be for us when you die.' ' Oh, no,' she joyously replied, ' you will see after my death I will let fall a shower of roses.'

Another time, when Mother Agnes was speaking to her in the same strain, she said : ' You will not have time to miss me. The postman will keep you so busy on my account.'

On July 16 Teresa made another prophetic announcement which has now become famous throughout the world. She turned to Mother Agnes and said : ' I feel that my Mission is soon to begin, to make others love God as I love Him . . . to teach souls my Little Way. Yes, I will spend my Heaven in doing good on earth.' ' What is the little way that you would teach to souls ? ' asked Mother Agnes. ' It is,' replied St.

Teresa, 'the Way of Spiritual Childhood, the way of trust and absolute self-surrender.'

A few days later another sister said to her : 'You will look down on us from Heaven.' She answered : 'No, I will come down and I will help priests, missionaries and the whole Church.'

We have seen how, when she was first asked to write the story of her life, she shrank from doing it and, though she did it under obedience, she said she would be quite willing to see it burnt. But on her sick bed her attitude changed completely. 'Mother,' she said, 'after my death my manuscript should not be spoken of to anyone until it is published. If you do otherwise or delay the publication the devil will set many snares for you in order to hinder God's good work, *a work that is very important.*' A few days after this, Mother Agnes gave the manuscript to little Teresa in order that she might revise a passage that seemed to her incomplete. Entering the infirmary soon afterwards she found the Saint with tears in her eyes and asked her why ? Teresa replied : 'It is indeed a manifestation of my soul. Yes, these pages will do a great deal of good. Through them God's tenderness and sweetness will become better known.' Then she added, in a tone which her sister never forgot : 'Yes, I know it, everyone will love me.'

St. Teresa now began to get rapidly worse. Her trials, physical and spiritual, became more acute. How did she meet them ? By being faithful to the Little Way and remaining always her Heavenly Father's little child. He was her Father, she was His child, therefore all was well.

Mother Agnes said to her one morning : ' Your sufferings are terrible ' ; to which she replied : ' No, they are not terrible. How can a victim of Love find anything terrible that is sent her by her Spouse ? At each moment He sends me what I am able to bear and nothing more. If He increases my pain He increases my strength as well. But I could never ask for greater suffering, for then it would be my own ; I should have to bear it without His help ; and I have never been able to do anything by myself.'

Here then is the answer. She was such a child, so little, that she let her Heavenly Father take her in His arms and carry her through it all. Her littleness was the secret of her strength and courage. The virtues of the Little Way shine out on her sick bed more brightly than ever before. Her love is invincible. ' He is free to do whatever He likes with me. I love all that He does.' Her humility and dependence upon her Father was complete. ' Oh, mother,' she said, ' what would become of me if God did not give me His strength ? How good God is in enabling me to bear all I suffer.' Her confidence is supreme. ' I have no fear of the last struggle, nor of the suffering, however great it is, of my sickness. God has helped me and guided me by His hand from my childhood's tenderest years. I am sure He will continue to help me to the end. I know very well that I may suffer very much, but never too much, of that I am sure.'

Always simple in her prayer, in her sickness she became simpler still. Apart from the Divine Office, which took about three hours and a quarter every day, it was not her custom to say long prayers, still less now. A simple child of Mary, she instinctively turns to her mother. 'Oh,' she said, 'if only you knew what this trial is like. This night, being unable to pray, I have just asked the Blessed Virgin to take my head in her hands so that I may be able to bear it.' Her devotion to Our Lady throughout her illness was very beautiful. 'Pray much to the Blessed Virgin for me,' she said ; 'if you were ill I should pray much for you.' When continuous prayers became impossible her childlike simplicity was never at a loss, and we get this exquisite incident. 'Being in great pain,' she told one of her sisters, 'I can only look at Our Blessed Lady and say "Jesus."' Her prayer consisted of countless little acts of love.

'Is it hard to suffer so much?' they asked her. 'No,' she replied, 'I am still able to tell God that I love Him, and that is enough.'

Later on she was at times unable even to do this. The infirmarian found her late one night with her hands joined and her eyes raised towards Heaven. 'What are you doing?' she asked her, 'you ought to get some sleep.' 'I cannot,

Sister,' she replied, ' I am suffering too much, so I pray.' ' What do you say to Jesus ? ' the sister asked her. ' I say nothing, I just love Him.'

Finally, unable to say her office, unable to meditate, unable to use her rosary, unable to formulate a single prayer, she says this lovely thing : ' What is my spiritual life in sickness ? ' you ask me. ' It is to suffer and that is all.' Instead of saying that all spiritual life was made impossible for her by her pain and disease, instead of being disheartened and depressed, she takes the only thing remaining, her suffering, and offers it to her Father in Heaven as proof of her love for Him and as a means of saving souls. And so her sickness becomes the expression of her love, becomes her Little Way to the Heart of her Heavenly Father and to the heart of all humanity, for whom she offers up her pain.

Thus does St. Teresa offer herself with the Divine Victim on the Cross. With Him she becomes a victim too. In so doing she shares His work of saving souls.

During these days she became so weak she could no longer make the smallest movement without help. She was suffering acutely from fever and could not say a word without pain.

To her great delight a little robin used to come and perch on the window-sill, and, looking this way and that, would after a little hesitation enter the sick room and flit about her bed. The evening before her death, about nine o'clock, little

Teresa and her sister Céline, who was sitting with her at the time, heard a sound of fluttering wings, and a dove—no one knew where it came from—alighted on the window-sill and remained there for a long time, cooing softly. This little incident gave Teresa great joy.

A little later, her sister Céline, bending over her, asked for a last message. Speaking with great difficulty and very faintly, little Teresa replied : ' It is love alone that counts.' She lingered on during another night. In the morning, casting a glance on the statue of the Blessed Virgin which was by her bed, she said : ' Oh, with what fervour I have prayed to her all night. But it was pure agony, without any consolation. Earth's air is failing me. When shall I breathe the air of Heaven ? ' Towards three o'clock she stretched her arms in the form of a cross. ' Mother,' she said to the Prioress, ' present me to the Blessed Virgin. Prepare me to die well.' Then, speaking very softly, she said : ' All that I have written of my desire for suffering is really true. I do not repent of having surrendered myself to Love.'

A little later she was heard to murmur : ' I would never have believed that it was possible to suffer so much, never, never ; I can only explain it by my intense desire to save souls.' Thus do we see the pain in that little cell of Carmel being offered for the salvation of souls and reaching to the very farthest corners of the world.

To cool her burning lips, her sister Céline bent down and refreshed them with a small piece of ice. A look of infinite tenderness and a smile of gratitude rewarded the ' little companion of her childhood ' for this last act of love.

Towards seven o'clock she turned to the Mother Prioress, saying : ' Am I not going to die ? ' The Mother Prioress replied : ' Yes, but perhaps not just yet.' ' Very well,' she murmured, ' let it be so. I would not wish to suffer less.' Then, fixing her eyes on her crucifix, she murmured : ' Oh . . . I LOVE HIM ! . . . MY GOD I . . . LOVE . . . THEE.' These were her last words. An act of supernatural love made completely in the dark. Slowly she fell back on the pillow. Then suddenly she raised herself up and opened her eyes, and in them there shone a joy and peace which her sisters say was too wonderful to be described by any human words ; then, with a look of wonder and radiant happiness she surrendered her soul into her Heavenly Father's arms, to the last His little child, the little victim of His Merciful Love.

CHAPTER SIX

ST. TERESA IN HEAVEN

THUS, on September 30, 1897, St. Teresa
died in the hiddenness of Carmel.

Four days afterwards the doors of Carmel were
opened and, with her sisters standing by, her body
was carried out over the threshold across which,
a short nine years before, she had stepped on the
day of her Clothing.

The funeral was very simple. The body was
carried on the workhouse hearse and was accom-
panied by a few priests and relations. The little
procession, in its simplicity, was typical of St.
Teresa and her Little Way. Led by the priests
they made their way up the beautiful Normandy
lane which leads from the town to the cemetery.
Here St. Teresa's body was laid to rest ; and the
mourners returned, thinking that the little sister's
work on earth was done. Outwardly it must have
seemed so.

But it was not so. During her illness St. Teresa
had said : ' I will spend my Heaven doing good
on earth.' Now we are going to see how all those
prophecies as to her future, which she made on
her sick bed, and which at the time seemed so

impossible, have been most wonderfully fulfilled by Almighty God.

When a nun dies in Carmel it is the custom for a little memoir of her life to be written and to be sent round to all the other Carmelite convents. In the case of St. Teresa the Mother Prioress decided that, instead of a memoir, they should send out the autobiography, the story of her life written by the Saint herself.

It was published during the month of October, within a few weeks of the Saint's death. The first edition consisted of two thousand copies, and one of the nuns, when she heard this, said : ' Whatever shall we do with these ? We shall have them all left on our hands.' She was wrong. From the very first the book had a marvellous sale. The various convents not only read it, but passed it on to their friends, and very soon the whole of France was talking of this marvellous book. In thirty-five years the number of copies sold had reached seven hundred thousand, while a shorter edition reached nothing less than two and a half million. It has been translated into more than thirty-five languages.

To-day this book is loved literally throughout the whole world. Pope Pius XI, speaking to all the faithful, said : ' The book on her own life, written by St. Teresa in the limpid beauty of her mother tongue in order to make known her Way of Spiritual Childhood, is not only in the hands of all, but its sweetness penetrates to hearts of men most estranged from Christian perfection ; numbers of them have been converted by reading it and are now firmly rooted in the charity of Christ.' And this was the little book which St. Teresa had to write just at odd moments, whenever she could find time in between her other duties, for she was given no special time in which to write it, the little book written amid interruptions and during an exhausting illness, written in just a penny copy-book, the little book of which St. Teresa foretold that the devil would set snares in order to hinder or delay its publication if it were not published at once, a prophecy which future events proved indeed to be true.

So Almighty God watched over the Mission of His Saint and preserved for all time those pages of which she said : ' These pages will do a great deal of good. Through them God's tenderness and sweetness will become better known.'

The autobiography spread rapidly throughout the world ; and wherever it was read the result was always the same. People immediately appealed to St. Teresa to help them in their need. The answer to these prayers was overwhelming. Sometimes it would be consolation and comfort for people in trouble, sometimes relief in sickness, sometimes courage to face some great temptation, sometimes for the grace of a happy death. Whatever it was St. Teresa came to their aid.

In every part of the world there happened miracles of healing. Sometimes it was the body that was healed of some terrible disease, or else it was the soul that was cured and sinners were brought back to the Church. In the mission field especially her supernatural power was seen. In answer to their prayers to her, missionaries were overwhelmed by people seeking the Sacraments of the Church.

Her miracles were mostly among the poor and humble and she seemed to have a special love for little children. But above all she lavished her love upon priests. She strengthened them in their labours, consoled them in their loneliness and comforted them in their sickness. Countless priests committed their priesthood to her care and were rewarded by supernatural blessings and wonders which they could only explain as her answer to their prayers. Many priests who had lost heart and grown weary found their early hopes re-kindled and their souls filled again with the Love of God. 'Pray to her,' said Pope Benedict XV to a priest, 'it is her vocation to teach priests to love Jesus Christ.'

Thus did St. Teresa scatter favours on the world, and thus did she fulfil her prophecy that she would scatter roses on the earth, a prophecy which, like the others, seemed, at the time it was made, to be so impossible.

To love, to be loved and to return to earth to make Love loved had been Teresa's great desire.

Pope Pius XI points this out : ' We have proof that, on entering Paradise, she began at once this work among souls when we see the mystical shower of roses which God permitted and still permits her to let fall on earth, as she had ingenuously foretold.' And again : ' We earnestly desire that all the faithful in Christ should prove themselves worthy of this abundant outpouring of grace, this mystical shower of roses which she scatters without ceasing.' No wonder the Holy Father called her a prodigy of miracles.

The result of this shower of roses was an immense number of letters to Carmel. The post soon became unmanageable. At the present moment the post at the Carmel at Lisieux averages three hundred letters a day, while if we include all the posts connected with Carmel received by the Office Centrale and the Director of Pilgrimages it reaches daily round about one thousand. Indeed her little mother, Mother Agnes, has been kept too busy to feel her loss, as the Saint foretold she would. Thus another of her prophecies which seemed impossible at the time has been actually fulfilled.

We have seen that St. Teresa, in her last illness, foretold that she would be loved by all the world. ' Yes, I know it,' she said, ' all the world will love me.' It was a strange thing for one so simple, so hidden, to say, but it was true ; her words were clearly inspired by Almighty God. For, in response to the shower of roses and to the love which the Saint poured out upon the whole world, there arose with startling rapidity a world-wide devotion to her and her Little Way.

Foremost among those who turned to her in love and confidence was Pope Pius XI. To her he turned in his many difficulties. He called her the 'beloved star of his Pontificate,' his 'consolation in all his trials.' Her statue was always on his writing table, just in front of him as he laboured throughout the day. And when, in his few free moments, he went into the garden in the Vatican City, he always knelt at the statue of the Saint which he had erected there. When the bishops came to pay their visits to him he used constantly to tell them : ' Pray to St. Teresa of the Child Jesus. We invoke her ceaselessly. Visit her sanctuary at Lisieux.'

Throughout the whole of Europe the devotion to her far surpassed the devotion to any other saint. Before long a statue of her was to be found in almost every church. It would be wearisome to count the different countries where she is honoured, for there is not one where she is not loved.

In America it was just the same, in the south as well as the north. In China, India, Japan, the Little Flower is everywhere to be found. Perhaps the most wonderful of all is the devotion that has arisen to her in Africa. Churches and seminaries there have been built in her honour. Missions have been founded and put under her protection. Hospitals, leper homes and whole dioceses have been dedicated to her.

Wherever the Catholic Church is found, and not only to the Catholics, but to many Protestants, Mohammedans and others she makes her marvellous appeal.

The humility of her life and the simplicity of her Little Way has literally taken the world by storm. There is no parallel in the history of the Church to this amazing devotion.

It was this universal and unparalleled devotion which led Pope Pius XI to declare her Patroness of the Missions and to describe her publicly as ' the child loved by all the world.' Thus the Church, through the voice of her Head, echoed the words spoken in the little Carmel cell and set its seal upon them as a prophecy divinely inspired by God.

Very soon the faithful throughout the world who, in their homes, had prayed to St. Teresa and received blessings in answer to their prayers, began to make their way to Lisieux to pray to her and to thank her at her very shrine. From the very first individuals had visited her grave. Individuals soon became groups, groups became hundreds and hundreds became thousands. By 1923 the pilgrims numbered fifty thousand a year. Her grave, which was quite simple and indistinguishable from all the rest, became a shrine for all the world. And this was while she was still simply Sister Teresa, for the Church had not yet spoken. During 1925, the year of her canonization, the number of pilgrims to Lisieux was three hundred and ten thousand. No fewer than four cardinals had knelt at the grave to ask her blessing, among them Cardinal Bourne, Archbishop of Westminster, who visited the grave in 1919. Bishops came in great numbers, priests and missionaries in thousands. Men and women of every station in life came with their sorrows and their joys, their hopes and their fears, their sickness and their suffering, to ask her help and comfort. It was life, with all its tragedy, that was to be seen, month after month, year after year, seeking Sister Teresa's simple grave.

In 1914 came the Great War. To the grave of Sister Teresa there now came a continual procession of soldiers, many of them wounded. In answer to their prayers many in the trenches were miraculously preserved by her from death. Those who were able to do so came to offer her their thanks and their devotion. Pope Benedict XV received so many letters from the trenches appealing to him to canonize Teresa that he did a most unusual thing and ordered a medal to be struck for the soldiers of her who was still only Sister Teresa.

All these events led the Holy See to hasten the canonization of little Teresa. All the world was asking that she should be proclaimed a saint.

Before this she must be beatified, for this is

the first stage in the Process of Canonization.
Owing to the world-wide demand this was done
with a rapidity literally unparalleled. Pope
Benedict XV, in order to hasten the Process,
dispensed with the fifty years which Canon Law
demands should intervene between death and
beatification. The first step was that the Pope
had to proclaim that Sister Teresa's virtue was
heroic. In signing this decree he said : ' In
spiritual childhood lies the secret of sanctity for
all the faithful. We desire that this secret should
be known to all our children.'

But before little Teresa could be beatified her
body had to be taken from the cemetery to the
Carmel and identified with solemn ceremony.
The day fixed for this was March 26, 1923. On
that spring morning over fifty thousand pilgrims
arrived in the town of Lisieux.

The grave was opened and the precious coffin
brought to the surface. As it was being lifted
from the grave the scent of roses coming from the
tomb was noticed by all standing near. The
coffin was then placed on a carriage draped in
white. Escorted by more than two hundred
priests, by the dignitaries of the town and by
thousands of the faithful, the procession made its
way along the same little Normandy lane up
which the body of Teresa had been carried in such
humble fashion some twenty-five years before.
Now it was being carried back in triumph.

It was a wonderful sight. No note of music

broke the silence, for the Church does not allow any public service or ceremony until the beatification has been officially pronounced. The only sound that could be heard was the murmuring of the Rosary by the faithful. As the coffin was carried past, a wounded soldier who had lost the use of both his legs recovered suddenly and completely ; while the eyes of a girl who was blind were opened to see the holy relics arrive at Carmel gate.

Here once more little Teresa's body was carried over the threshold of Carmel to be received by her three sisters, who had parted from it with such sorrow only twenty-six years before.

In January, 1922, Pope Benedict XV died and Pope Pius XI was his successor. On April 29, 1923, he, as Head of the Church, declared Teresa to be one of the Blessed in Heaven. In St. Peter's, in the presence of forty-five archbishops and bishops, together with a great multitude of the faithful, the Pontifical Brief was read. Its subject was the Little Way of Spiritual Childhood, of which Teresa was proclaimed by the Church to be a teacher for all the faithful.

In order to meet the public demand for her canonization, Pope Pius XI, like his predecessor, dispensed with the long delay which the Canonical Statutes demand between beatification and canonization. The Statutes, he said, must yield ' to the supplication of the whole Catholic world.'

The day chosen for this great triumph was May 17, 1925. The scene in St. Peter's baffles description. Never had such an assembly gathered at any canonization before ; it was probably the largest and most distinguished gathering that had been seen beneath the dome of Michael Angelo for centuries. Thirty-four cardinals were present. Over two hundred archbishops and bishops followed in the procession. Innumerable prelates, representatives of the religious orders, priests and missionaries in their hundreds walked behind them. When they had passed to their seats, there came the splendid banner with the picture of the Saint. Then came the entry of the Holy Father. Slowly, in the midst of this magnificent throng, hailed with enthusiasm by over forty thousand of the faithful, he was borne to the splendid throne erected in front of St. Peter's chair.

The moment had come to declare solemnly before the whole Church the entry of little Teresa into the glory of Heaven. The invocation of the Holy Ghost was repeated ; and then came the solemn words : ' Arise, Peter is about to speak by the mouth of Pius.' A tense silence held captive that tremendous throng. Seated on the chair of Peter, Pius XI, his face radiant with joy, pronounced the formula which was to send heavenwards a fervent Hosanna from the Universal Church : ' We declare Blessed Teresa of the Child Jesus to be a Saint. We define that such she is. . . . In the Name of the Father and of the Son and of the Holy Ghost. Amen.' The infallible teacher had spoken. Immediately there burst forth the exultant tones of the silver trumpets. The bells of St. Peter's pealed, and with their deep notes were mingled those of the bells of every church in the Eternal City. The acclamations of the thousands in the basilica swelled into one great thunder of applause which was taken up by the two hundred thousand waiting in the square outside. Never had there been such a canonization as this.

After the Gospel, the Holy Father pointed out to the whole Catholic Church the reason of this canonization. It was in order to exalt St. Teresa before the whole world as the teacher of the Little Way of Spiritual Childhood. His homily ended with the ringing words : ' We desire most earnestly that all the faithful should study her in order to copy her, becoming children themselves, since otherwise they cannot, according to the word of the Master, arrive at the Kingdom of Heaven. If this Way of Spiritual Childhood were to be universally followed, who can fail to see how easily would be realized that reformation of human society which We set ourselves to accomplish at the commencement of Our pontificate ? '

Here then, in the basilica of St. Peter's, in a scene of unparalleled splendour, through the mouth of the Supreme Head of the Church on earth speaking to all the faithful, is the fulfilment of those simple words, spoken but twenty-eight years before in the hiddenness of a Carmel cell by the unknown dying nun : ' I feel that my mission is about to begin, my mission of teaching souls, my Little Way, the Little Way of Spiritual Childhood.'

That afternoon the Holy Father spoke for the space of an hour to the Cardinal Archbishop of Philadelphia on the subject of ' his first saint,' and confessed to him that never in his life had he felt so happy as he felt that day in the wonderful glorification of the little Saint, ' whom you in America call the Little Flower, but whom I call my Guiding Star.'

That night the streets were thronged with pilgrims as well as with the Roman people, watching a spectacle that had not been revived since 1870.

The gigantic cupola, the Basilica façade, and even the double colonnade of the great square of St. Peter's were illuminated by thousands of torches which marked out their architecture in lines of light, throwing the reflection far away, even over the distant waters of the Tiber.

' God's glory, that is my only ambition. My own I abandon to Him.' So she had written in the hiddenness of Carmel. Out of that hiddenness the Heavenly Father that day lifted her with a triumph quite unique in the history of the Church, so that, through her, souls in their thousands might be drawn to love Him as she did, whose one aim had ever been ' to love Jesus and to make Him loved.'

The day following, the Holy Father gave a special audience to the pilgrims from France. ' Few saints,' he said to them, ' have been God's privileged ones to the same degree as your dear little saint. Let your lives be your thanksgiving to her who from the cloister offers us an example of perfection that everyone can and should imitate. She desires to draw us along her Little Way. Her Little Way is beautiful, fruitful, and safe. It is a way of peace and holiness, a new omen to the world, *omen novum*.' The Holy Father concluded by saying that her feast would never be forgotten for ' even this Eternal City is not accustomed to such wonders.'

Rome had exalted Teresa with, to use the Holy Father's own words, ' a hurricane of glory.'

'OH, My God, I desire to love Thee and to make Thee loved—I wish to labour for Thy love alone, with the sole aim of pleasing Thee, of consoling Thy Sacred Heart and of saving souls who will love Thee through all Eternity. In order that my life may be one act of perfect love I offer myself as a victim to Thy Merciful Love.'

In these words St. Teresa sums up the whole of her vocation. We have seen how, from a tiny child, she was taught by her mother to love God above everything else and to seek to grow in love through little sacrifices. We saw how the mother gave the little one a chaplet of beads in order that she might count these little sacrifices as she made them.

Thus she learnt that it is by little sacrifices alone that love can grow, that it is by little sacrifices all day long that we are freed from our self-love and can grow in love for God and love for those around us for His sake.

We have seen how in Carmel God led her along this path till gradually through the continual sacrifice of herself in little things her soul was so purified from all self-love that she was able to

offer her life to Him in one act of perfect love ;
so that Our Lord was able to take her right into
the heart of His work of saving souls and that is
why St. Teresa is now loved by souls throughout
the whole Catholic world.

St. Teresa ends her autobiography with the
prayer : ' O Jesus, I entreat Thee to let Thy
Divine eyes rest upon a vast number of little
souls. I entreat Thee to choose in this world a
legion of little victims of Thy Love.' Pope
Pius XI, at the end of his address to the whole
Church at the canonization of the Saint, repeats
her very words : ' We therefore adopt as our
own,' he said, ' the prayer of the new St. Teresa
with which she ends her invaluable autobiography : " O Jesus, I entreat Thee to let
Thy Divine eyes rest upon a vast number of
little souls. I entreat Thee to choose in this
world a legion of little victims of Thy Love." '
Clearly the Holy Father desires us to follow in
her steps.

In the Mass of St. Teresa our mother the
Church says this beautiful prayer : ' May the
heavenly mystery inflame us with that fire of
love whereby Thy virgin Saint, Teresa, offered
herself to Thee as a victim of charity for all
mankind ; through Our Lord Jesus Christ.'
Thus our mother the Church, too, prays that
many of her children will follow in the steps of
St. Teresa in their love for God.

With our mother the Church calling us to

follow St. Teresa and giving us grace that we may be able to do so, let us generously answer to that call, and let us too labour. Not one of us need be afraid to answer that call, not one of us need hesitate to follow her along the Little Way of Spiritual Childhood, to labour for the love of Jesus alone, with the sole aim of pleasing Him, of consoling His Sacred Heart and of saving souls who will love Him for all Eternity. But to do this we must become as little children, for ' *unless you be converted and become as little children you shall not enter the Kingdom of Heaven.*'

THE END